EVER~~YTHING~~
FATHER OF
THE BRIDE
BOOK

A survival guide for Dad!

Shelly Hagen

Adams Media
Avon, Massachusetts

For my Dad, our family's very own Great One

An Everything® Series Book.
Everything® and everything.com are registered trademarks of
F+W Publications, Inc.

Published by Adams Media, an F+W Publications Company
57 Littlefield Street, Avon, MA 02322 U.S.A.
www.adamsmedia.com

ISBN 10: 1-59337-148-9
ISBN 13: 978-1-59337-148-7

Printed in Canada.
J I H G F E D C

Library of Congress Cataloging-in-Publication Data
Hagen, Shelly.
The everything father of the bride book / Shelly Hagen.
        p.   cm.
ISBN 1-59337-148-9
1. Weddings–Planning. 2. Wedding etiquette. 3. Brides–Family relationships.
4. Fathers and daughters. I. Title. II. Series: Everything series.

HQ745.H182 2004
395.2'2–dc22

2004013355

This publication is designed to provide accurate and authoritative information
with regard to the subject matter covered. It is sold with the understanding that
the publisher is not engaged in rendering legal, accounting, or other professional
advice. If legal advice or other expert assistance is required, the services of a
competent professional person should be sought.

—From a *Declaration of Principles* jointly adopted by a Committee of the
American Bar Association and a Committee of Publishers and Associations

Many of the designations used by manufacturers and sellers to distinguish their
products are claimed as trademarks. Where those designations appear in this
book and Adams Media was aware of a trademark claim, the designations have
been printed with initial capital letters.

This book is available at quantity discounts for bulk purchases.
For information, call 1-800-289-0963.

THE

EDITORIAL

Publishing Director: Gary M. Krebs
Managing Editor: Kate McBride
Copy Chief: Laura MacLaughlin
Acquisitions Editors: Bethany Brown and Kate Burgo
Development Editor: Christina MacDonald
Production Editor: Bridget Brace, Jamie Wielgus

PRODUCTION

Production Director: Susan Beale
Production Manager: Michelle Roy Kelly
Series Designer: Daria Perreault
Cover Design: Paul Beatrice, Matt LeBlanc
Layout and Graphics: Colleen Cunningham,
Rachael Eiben, Michelle Roy Kelly,
John Paulhus, Daria Perreault, Erin Ring

Visit the entire Everything® series at www.everything.com

Contents

Acknowledgments

I want to thank the women who helped in getting this book off the ground and who also helped me whip it into shape: my agent, Jessica Faust; and Bethany Brown and Kate Burgo at Adams. Thanks to my dad for providing such great fodder for this project with his antics during my sister's and my weddings; and thanks to the dads who were under my microscope as they worked their ways through their daughters' engagements and/or weddings. A front row seat to someone else's learning experience is priceless.

The Top Ten Errors Made by Uninformed Fathers of the Bride

1. Saying, "Whatever you want, honey," to the bride.
2. Selling the car to pay for the wedding.
3. Not trying on the tux before bringing it home.
4. *Wearing* the incorrect, ill-fitting, powder blue tux . . . because it doesn't look *that* bad.
5. Leaving the unibrow as-is.
6. Engaging in a battle of wits with the groom-to-be to show him who's who and what's what.
7. Pulling the Invisible Man act at the reception.
8. Expecting too much maturity from the newlyweds.
9. Expecting *no* maturity from the newlyweds.
10. Leading the bachelor party mayhem.

Introduction

FATHER OF THE BRIDE—the very words conjure up an image of a dapper dad in his tuxedo, ready and waiting to walk his daughter down the aisle. Some people, of course, think of a man furiously signing checks made out to the caterer, the baker, the band, the florist . . . .

No matter what the words mean to you, you've been playing the role since your daughter announced her engagement. There's more to this character, though, than the tux and the checkbook. You'll soon find out that one of your responsibilities—as important as walking her down the aisle—is offering a shoulder to cry on when the planning gets hectic; another is communicating with your family, with whom you may have been out of touch for eons before this wedding threatened to gather you all together under the same roof sometime next June.

If this is your first time in the wedding planning arena, you may have absolutely no idea what's expected of you—financially or otherwise. Are you really supposed to pay for every single wedding-related expense? Will you have to buy your own tuxedo? Do you have to go to your future son-in-law's bachelor party? And what about your ex-wife, her new husband, your new wife, and all the stepkids? Where does everyone fit into the wedding diagram?

Weddings have come a long way since the first etiquette books were written, so if you've received most of your information from these sources, you can relax. For the most part, when they were published, societal rules were very rigid and didn't account for any situations other than what was deemed "proper"; divorce, remarriage, and single parenting were never mentioned. Fortunately, nothing is off limits today—families come in such varied structures, and more and more brides (and grooms) are throwing etiquette to the wind and relying on their own common sense.

So where does the father of the bride fit into all of this? Anywhere you want to, anywhere you're welcome to, and anywhere it makes sense for you to. If your daughter wants your complete involvement and you have the time and resources to offer, grab the chance. Though it's true that a daughter is a daughter all of her life, she'll also be a wife soon—which means that her first priority will be her husband. If you have an opportunity to help her plan her wedding, you'll be left with priceless memories of time well spent together.

Of course, you'll probably be called on to whip out that checkbook, but before you reach for the antacids, realize that many, many young couples pay for at least part of their own weddings these days, and unless you've been telling your daughter that you'll foot the bill for everything, you may not have to.

Your best bet for a happy, mostly problem-free, pre-wedding season? Communication. Don't be afraid to ask questions (of your daughter, of the caterer, of the groom, of *whomever*); don't be afraid to express your feelings (if you feel that 600 guests is too many, say so—nicely); and don't hold back the urge to tell your daughter that you're proud of the woman she's become and that you're happy for her. She may already know it, but she needs to hear it from her dad.

Chapter 1
Daddy's Little Girl

Your daughter has just come sweeping through the door with a man in tow and announced that she's engaged. Your first reaction? "No way. Not gonna happen. This man is robbing the cradle." Hang on there, Dad. Is it possible that your baby girl is all grown up? (And is it just as possible that she's chosen a great man to spend the rest of her life with?) It might just be that you need to learn to let go of her . . . a little.

She's No Bride, She's a Kid!

Having a hard time even *thinking* about your daughter leaving your nest in order to make a nest with someone else? You're not alone. Many fathers feel the same way, especially if their daughter has heretofore not shown a great deal of get-up-and-go. If she's been perfectly content to live in your house, eat your food, and hit you up for fifty bucks every weekend, you might have a *lot* of reservations about her decision to get married. After all, you're thinking, she has no idea what it's like out there.

Or maybe your daughter is the exact opposite: she left home as soon as she could and was always incredibly independent, but suddenly, she's talking about acquiring a husband and a permanent address. She's only had to worry about herself up 'til now. You see this ending badly. How can you make sure she knows what she's getting into? (That's your *job* after all, isn't it?)

Of course, your daughter may be dealing with other life issues at this point, such as a remarriage or how to announce her engagement to her kids. If this sounds like your situation, flip to Chapter 8 for some helpful advice. Dads who are new to this topic, read on . . .

Give Her Some Credit

Your concerns may be valid, of course, but the crux of the issue is whether your daughter understands the seriousness and the size of the commitment she's about to make. Although it is, in fact, your job to guide her and to help her make the right decisions in life, it is not your job to tell her what she can and can't do in her adult life. You can't expect her to ever reach maturity if you're calling all the shots, no matter how good your intentions are.

If your daughter isn't quite taking the world by storm, but she does show signs of inching toward a deeper understanding of life (she knows, for example, that holding down a steady job is a definite bonus, and that buying twenty pairs of shoes in one afternoon is a definite no-no), she's probably already more grown up than you think. She may be young, she may even be a little silly, but she's got a brain up there (and she probably inherited your common sense, even if she hates to admit it—or show it).

 FACT

> Remember: Just about everyone grows up at some point, and marriage may be just the thing to take your daughter from *almost*-adulthood into the real thing, precisely because there's no safety net. Her marriage will be her responsibility; *you* can't be the one picking up the pieces.

She's Old Enough to Vote

Of course, many fathers panic when their youngish daughters have a whirlwind courtship and lightning-quick engagement. Actually, these same dads would probably be uncomfortable with the whole setup if they had known the prospective groom for five years. The issue here is their daughter's age. These dads lose sleep thinking about the myriad of possibilities: How can a girl who has just barely finished college (or hasn't yet) even *think* about marriage? She has her whole life ahead of her; she should be thinking about having some fun before she settles down.

Well, that decision isn't really yours to make. If everything else in the picture seems up to snuff (she's marrying a nice guy, and they have a plan as far as where they're going to live and how they're going to pay the bills), there isn't a whole lot to complain about. Keep in mind that somewhere, another father is experiencing the agony of watching his career-minded, well-off, thirtysomething daughter marry some creep because she wants to have a husband before she's forty.

 ALERT!

Unless you're dealing with a sixteen-year-old daughter who is bound and determined to elope with her fifty-year-old, long-haired (and extremely *cool*) garage-band boyfriend, her age shouldn't be your primary concern.

She does have her whole life ahead of her: She's chosen to share it with a hardworking, decent man. Be happy that *she's* happy, even if you wish she would bum around Europe with her friends instead of getting hitched.

A Little Overprotective, Are Ya?

The mere mention of your name makes the boyfriends shake. The sound of your voice sends them running. If it were up to you (and your wife), your daughter would be living in an ivory tower. She's much too fragile to handle what the world has to offer, and you, quite frankly, can't bear the thought of her having to suffer through life's tough lessons. You'll take care of her by sheltering her.

Sound familiar? Are you constantly being told that you're way too overprotective? That if you don't cool it, your kids will never know anything about (or be able to handle) real life? Take this little quiz to find out where you fall in the scheme of fatherly surveillance. Be honest. Although many of these questions will refer to your daughter's childhood, you're looking for a pattern of behavior that you might very well be carrying on today without realizing it.

1. As a toddler, your daughter:
   a. Played with the neighborhood kids at their houses.
   b. Played at your home with neighborhood kids.
   c. Wasn't allowed to play with the neighborhood ruffians.

Now, you might have lived in a tough neighborhood, and maybe in that case, you were right to keep your kids at home—alone. But if you were living in a decent area and your main fears were all about what could happen . . . that's being overprotective.

2. As children, your kids were in the Emergency Room for:

a. Every cold, fever, and hangnail.

b. Broken bones and deep wounds.

c. You'd never let them into that germ-laden environment.

Hmm . . . if you're answering a or c . . . that's overprotective parenting.

3. When your daughter first started talking about boys, your reply was:

a. "Boys are bad! Stay away!"

b. A reluctant, "All right . . . let's hear about these boys."

c. Your daughter knows better than to bring up the topic around you.

Obviously, the only nonoverprotective answer is b. If you tried (a), to steer your daughter away from boys (because you were one once, after all, and you know what they're all about) to the point that (c) she knew better than to even suggest that she had a boyfriend . . . that's being overprotective.

4. As a teenager, your daughter was:

a. Rebellious

b. Quiet

c. Right next to you and your wife all the time.

If your teenage daughter never left the house, it might be because she was shy or because she was a homebody. But if she was never allowed to leave because you were too afraid of what might happen to her if she did . . . you were being overprotective.

5. When your daughter chose a college, you made sure it was:
   a. The best you could afford.
   b. Able to meet her needs—athletic, artistic, etc.
   c. Right around the block. College campuses are dangerous places.

While it's completely understandable that you'd want your child to be safe, keeping her at arm's length isn't the only way to do this. In fact, if you've never let her out of your sight, you've kind of set her up for a lifetime of depending on you . . . which is being overprotective.

6. In college, your daughter brought home her boyfriends for the weekend.
   a. True
   b. False

Assuming your daughter had a few significant others over the course of her college years, one or two of them probably made an appearance at your dinner table . . . unless, of course, you made no bones about the fact that college men are only after one thing. That, by the way, is being overprotective.

7. Your daughter's boyfriend, James, has just asked for your permission to marry her. In response, you said:

   a. "Tell me about your plans for the future, Jimbo."

   b. "Get out of my house!"

   c. "I gotta tell you, Jim, that you aren't really my daughter's type. She likes much taller, smarter, richer men. So that settles that."

Raking James over the coals a bit (a) is perfectly acceptable, as long as you don't make him cry. Ordering him out of your home (b), or making him feel as though he's not worthy of your princess (c) is being overprotective.

8. Your daughter is talking about this wonderful man she's met and how she thinks he might be The One. Your first thought:

   a. No thoughts. You choose to roll your eyes instead.

   b. "He's probably just going to break her heart."

   c. "Great! Look how happy she is!"

Answering b? That's being overprotective, considering you haven't met the guy yet. Reserve your judgment until you've sat down and really talked with him. Then you're free to make an honest evaluation of his character.

9. She's bound and determined to marry this guy. Your last resort is to:

a. Accept it and support her decision.

b. Have him checked out.

c. Pay this guy off so that he leaves town.

Having the guy checked out isn't actually that bad— it borders on being insanely overprotective, but if he's given you legitimate reasons to question his character (he freely admits to laundering money, for example), it's not such a crazy thing to do. Paying him off, on the other hand, is a bad move . . . and it's definitely crossing the line into overprotective territory.

10. Your daughter has taken her vows, she's back from the honeymoon, and she's in tears. Apparently, she's having second thoughts. You:

a. Clear out her old room and insist that she come home. You were right!

b. Tell her to find her husband and work things out.

c. Hand her over to her mother—you don't know how to handle this.

Every marriage has its ups and downs. If you didn't approve of the wedding in the first place, resisting the urge to take care of everything for your emotional daughter is difficult. Chances are, she'll work things out. . . . If you've been shouting, "Leave him! Leave him!" you're going to appear—what's the word?—overprotective.

So What *Is* Your Role?

Your role in your adult child's life is to support her, love her, and listen to her. Sure, you can offer advice; of course you can be (diplomatically) honest about what you really think of someone or of a situation. But that's where your role comes to an end and your daughter's *life* begins. You can't (or shouldn't) run her life, and you can't (or shouldn't) pick up the pieces of her misadventures.

 ESSENTIAL

Think back to your own coming-of-age: How did you learn the most valuable lessons in life? By taking care of business *yourself*. Many fathers don't want to see their kids go through the same tough times as they did, but while the sentiment is lovely, the long-term effects are not.

Kids who've never had to pay their own way never learn the value of money. Kids who've never had to live by the same rules as everyone else often end up in situations that they just can't get out of without your help, and are sometimes despised by those who *do* have to fend for themselves. You can do a lot of things for your little girl; unfortunately, taking the knocks of everyday life isn't one of those things.

The Gift of a Real-World Education

If she's still young enough to be somewhat dependent on you and her mother *and* she's talking about getting married, your major concern is how the heck this kid is going to take care of herself and a husband. You can help her learn the basics before she's out on her own by sitting down and going over a few money matters.

Be Tough

Tough love is a tough thing to carry through on. If you're very concerned about how she and her new husband will pay the bills (because neither of them seem to know the first thing about money or budgeting), it's important for you to provide her with a crash-course in budgeting, *before* her credit is ruined by an inability to pay her bills once she's out on her own.

 ALERT!

Getting tough on the money issue differs wildly from being overprotective, by the way. In this situation, you're actually giving her the tools to survive out there in the world; you're not taking care of the bills for her. Don't feel guilty for taking the lead on this topic.

If she starts crying and tells you that you're the meanest dad in the whole world, then you'll know you were right to carry on with this experiment. This is something that's imperative to her happy, successful future: Many young couples break up over money (when the issue of who's spending how much on what crops up, or, worse yet, when the realization that life really stinks when you're broke makes its entrance into a new marriage). The better she understands the value of budgeting before she flies the coop, the better off she'll be in the long run.

Run Through the Budget

If you've been taking care of the finances for her entire life, your daughter may not have the slightest idea of whom you write checks to every month, or how much money you actually spend when you pay the bills. Sit down with her (and her paycheck stub) and go through a typical month of bills, estimating what she's likely to pay for things where you don't have an actual number. This list might include the following:

- Food
- Rent
- Transportation (car payments, maintenance, commuting expenses)
- Utilities (gas, water, electric, cable, heat, garbage)
- Credit card
- Other outstanding debt (student loans)

These are the bare minimum expenses of life. These payments don't include anything fun—aside from the credit card, which, you should mention, should be used only when absolutely necessary.

Explain that it's always best to pay cash, and if she uses her credit card frequently, she should keep track of her purchases and pay them off at the end of each month. Explain to her that carrying a balance means that she's likely paying somewhere in the vicinity of 19 percent on the outstanding debt.

Hand Over the Bills

If she's living with you and you're not making her pay rent or utilities, now's a good time to start, especially if she's never lived anywhere *but* home. Since these expenses will eat up a good chunk of her paycheck, it's important for her to realize it now—before she ties the knot and realizes that, yes, housing is expensive, and so is food, and so is heat . . . and there isn't a whole lot of room to cut back on some of these expenses.

Anybody Have Some Ibuprofen?

So, what if you're not particularly overprotective of your kids and you've never given them a free ride on the rent? Does that mean that you're poised to accept anything that's thrown your way? Maybe not. What if your daughter comes home with a man who is the complete opposite of the husband you had in mind for her? What if, for that matter, she seems to have completely lost her mind and seems to have chosen this unlikely candidate simply because she knew that you and her mother would disapprove? What if she wants to plan a wedding that you think is absolutely crazy? What are your rights as a father then? (You *do* have some rights here, don't you?)

Mr. Wrong

If your daughter brings home a fiancé who is obviously (to you, anyway) not her type, take the time to assess what she really sees in him. If she's always been rebellious, her engagement to a man who seems to be all wrong for her may be a continuation of her rather adolescent behavior. If, on the other hand, she's always been levelheaded, it's unlikely that she would deliberately chose an unsuitable mate just to make you crazy. He might have a few hidden layers that aren't visible to you just yet.

 FACT

> Whoever said love conquers all had the right idea—he just didn't allow for situations where the love is actually more like infatuation. Your daughter may well cling to this man more if you threaten to disown her for marrying him.

Another thing to think about is how long she's known this guy. If they've been dating for a year, chances are she's put some thought into this decision, and you should defer to her best judgment. You may still have your reservations, but you're not in the relationship—you can't make a fair evaluation without all the evidence, which you don't have. On the other hand, if she's been dating this guy for two weeks and she's announced that they're getting married in a month . . . you're right to worry.

In either event, though, you risk pushing her away from you and your guidance if you come on too strong. Your situation here is not easy; no one would tell you that it is. You don't have to sit back and smile and nod—make your concerns known, but do it tactfully. (Don't, for example, use the words *stupid* and *jerkface* to describe the man she plans to marry.) You don't have to pay for the wedding if you feel as though the whole thing is a sham. If your daughter is hell-bent on marrying this guy, she will, whether you approve or not, and whether you foot the bill or not.

The Artistic Wedding

Your daughter and future son-in-law are so creative. They want to have a nudist wedding, during which they will exchange vows in the buff. The preacher will be baring all, the attendants will be au naturel . . . and you're expected to pay for this, and to invite your family? *No way*, you say.

Hopefully, your daughter won't ask you to attend her wedding wearing nothing but a smile, but a lot of engaged women are looking to plan unusual ceremonies and receptions—the plans for which might leave you feeling shaken. You were thinking a couple of hundred people, the country club, and a big wedding cake; your daughter is thinking several hundred people, a circus tent, and cotton candy booths (oh, and acrobats and mimes). How do you insert your own preferences without coming off as controlling?

If you will not pay for the circus tent wedding, you need to lay that on the table (and the sooner the better) so that your daughter can get angry, get over it, and find another place—or so that she (and the groom) can find another way to finance the big wedding.

Don't expect her to completely conform to tradition, and don't insist that she do things exactly the way you want them done. Here's where the art of compromise comes into play. The two of you will have to find a happy middle ground—something that will make her happy (it is *her* wedding after all), and something that you and your guests will feel comfortable with. That's only fair, and it's the way adults work things out together.

She *Is* All Grown Up

No matter how you feel about the matter, sooner or later your daughter is going to reach a point where she can't reasonably be referred to as a kid anymore. She's probably getting close to that point as you sit and read this. You have to learn to see her as an adult and appreciate her unique take on things, especially if she's contemplating marriage.

If you can sit down and talk to her about her plans while treating her like an adult, you're much more likely to hear how she really feels. (Is she a little scared? Does she feel overwhelmed?) These are areas where you might be able to offer her some real insight and invaluable guidance if you're willing to talk to her in a way that lets her know you know she has a brain in her head.

ALERT!

> Telling her that she's too young to get married is going to light a fire in her belly. She knows she's not too young to commit to her man, and you're setting up a game of one-upman-ship. (She'll prove to you that she's serious by marrying him, see?)

Too many fathers—with the best of intentions—make the mistake of distancing themselves from their almost-adult daughters because deep down, they think that parenting a young woman is really a job for her mother. Not true. Any girl who has a good relationship with her father will appreciate his take on life. She may not follow your advice in the end, but the fact that you've taken the time to really talk to her as a grownup will take your relationship from the sandbox into the real world.

Keep an Open Mind

You know your daughter may not have made the choices you would like to have seen her make, but she's getting there. To judge her negatively based on the fact that she forged her own trail instead of following a map that a certain father of hers tried to give her is unfair. Be aware of the common things that convince parents (wrongly) that their children are not now, nor will they ever be, adult enough to be married.

The Career Scene

You wanted her to go to law school, or at the very least, get her MBA. She could be making a killing on Wall Street, or she could be tearing witnesses up on the stand every day. Instead, she chose to work in a coffee house. Jeepers creepers, you think, did I teach her nothing about life? How's she going to make it on minimum wage?

 FACT

Consider how difficult it was for her to *not* follow the path you laid out for her—the sure thing. She would, no doubt, be making a good living if she had gone to graduate school. Obviously, what matters more to her is achieving success on her own terms; she also wants to succeed doing something she enjoys.

Do you have any idea what her interests are? It could well be that she is planning on one day opening up her own little café or becoming a chef or a caterer, and this job is a stepping stone (and a learning experience) for her.

Think of it this way: Pick something that you do for fun or relaxation or simply because you're good at it. Is it the same thing you do for a living? If you could make money doing it, would you? If you were thirty years younger, would you take that shot?

Be honest. You'll see that she's not so silly after all. She might even know exactly what she's doing, and she might be the one laughing all the way to the bank someday.

Previous Relationships

Yes, she's brought home some doozies in the boyfriend department. There was that guy who was conducting a sensory-deprivation experiment and so chose not to open his eyes for the entire weekend; and then there was that other guy who was forever singing show tunes—loudly and off-key and at the most inappropriate moments (hey, he *honestly* thought that Aunt Betty's wake could use a little jazzing up). And what about the guy who was convinced that he was an illegitimate member of a certain royal family because of his uncanny resemblance to a particular prince? As you recall, he was off to Europe to claim his birthright . . .

So she's made some curious relationship choices in the past. That doesn't mean that *any* relationship of hers is bound to involve a young man of questionable intelligence. Just as it isn't fair to compare your future son-in-law to any other sons-in-law you may have, it isn't fair to judge him against your daughter's former beaus. She may have actually found a winner this time.

ALERT!

Yes, everyone knows that as the family patriarch, you know best, and your predictions usually come to fruition. Consider, though, that you may be a bit prejudiced, confusing your daughter's fiancé with those who have gone before. Give the guy a fair shake—it's what you'd want if you were in his shoes.

Her Support System

Your daughter is your baby—and not necessarily because you want it that way. She simply can't function without touching base with you or your wife several times a day; there's no way she can deal with life without you holding her hand. And now she says she's getting married. You can see it now: You'll be supporting her, her husband, and their kids.

Here's where letting go becomes your priority. If she's planning on getting married and leaving the nest, you have to help her to do it. Acknowledge that she's made a life-changing decision. As long as the boyfriend seems like a decent enough bloke, it's *really* all right for you to let go of the past and start thinking that she just may be headed for matrimonial bliss.

In any event, reminding her that she's never been able to make it on her own won't help matters and is not the helpful criticism that you might think it is. (In fact, it's just cruel.) This man in her life may be the self-esteem booster she's been needing all of these years, so don't assume the worst—help her to help herself. Be the strong, supportive (and if you can't say anything positive, *silent*) father of the bride.

So You're Flying Solo

Not only is she all you have, you're all that she has had; up 'til now, anyway. As a single dad you're playing the role of dad *and* mom to your daughter due to divorce or death. Whatever the case, if you long ago assumed complete responsibility for this child, you've taken the role very seriously. The discussion about *other* Fathers of the Bride doesn't really relate to your situation, because, quite frankly, you have more to think about than the dads who are simply going to walk their daughters down the aisle.

 ESSENTIAL

Taking care of a child on your own is no small task. Of course, the benefit is that you may have developed a much closer relationship with your daughter than you might have otherwise had . . . which makes handing her off to a groom *that* much more difficult.

Realize that your daughter probably feels as protective of you as you do of her. She's not going to sprint down the aisle and out of your life; she's simply maturing and stepping into a fuller life, one that she's going to include you in. The alternative to this is her staying single forever—a viable choice for a woman who *wants* to be single, but a lonely choice for someone who dreams of having her own family.

Try not to think of her wedding in terms of her leaving you. You'll find (after the wedding) that your fears are unfounded, that you haven't lost a daughter— and that you really have *gained* a son-in-law.

Chapter 2

Your Future Son-in-Law

What if you could list the characteristics that you would prefer in the new man entering your family fold—would he be intelligent, wealthy, honest, ambitious? Hmm . . . what about the things that your daughter would prefer in a husband (namely someone with a sense of humor and that rather ambiguous trait, *potential*)? If you already have a son-in-law who's great (because he's just like *you*), you might have some pretty high (and unfair) standards for the new guy. Give him a fair chance, Dad.

The Blessing

If you've merely been the figurehead of the household (your wife is really running the show, although she occasionally yields to you on some issues that she doesn't want to deal with, and the kids know that she's the one to ask for, well, *anything*), it may seem strange to you that your future son-in-law would want your blessing to marry your daughter. After all, she's pretty much done what she's wanted all of her life; why should anything change now?

On the flip side, if you've been very close to your daughter and very involved in her life, you might require that this young man come to you on bended knee to ask for your daughter's hand in marriage. And you have no intention of giving it easily.

 FACT

This is one of the big Dad Moments of the wedding season (and there aren't *that* many). The focus is on you and your reaction to this young man's inquiry. Sure, you can fluff it off with a simple nod of authorization . . . *or* you can seize the moment.

Whatever your position in the family, your daughter's beau may request your permission to marry her, especially if your daughter is a fairly traditional type of girl.

If she's a firm believer in this particular tradition, she'll instruct her boyfriend on how to proceed with you; on the other hand, if she thinks this custom is a bunch of hooey, she'll simply come home one day and announce her engagement.

You might come from a generation or a family that didn't believe in this particular custom. You might just think it's a formality, and no matter what you say, she's going to marry this guy anyway, so what's the point?

The point is that this little conversation is the perfect time to have any of your questions answered. So if you don't have any right now and you sense that this little chat is on the horizon, come up with a few, for kicks if for nothing else. This young man will have worked up his courage to come and address this topic with you—make it worth his while.

Get Down to It

You might have some very valid concerns about this man's plans for the future. If, for example, he's still a student and your daughter is going to support him throughout the remainder of his schooling, you have every right to ask how he's going to return the favor once he's out of the academic world. (Will she have to continue working sixty hours a week for the next ten years to pay off his student loans? Does he plan on going on for *another* degree after he finishes this one? In the end, are these useful, money-earning degrees, or will the two of them struggle to make ends meet for the next fifty years?)

If you're getting answers that disturb you (he's telling you, for example, that even though they're broke, they're going to have a family right away, and they figure that down the road, everything will take care of itself), you're right to voice your concerns. You do have a lot of life experience, after all, and you might just be the voice of reason to this man who may not have anyone else to look to for advice.

 ESSENTIAL

Feel free to ask the probing questions: Where are they planning on living after the wedding? Can they afford to get married right now? What about kids? Are they going to wait until they can support them before they start their family?

Do the Numbers—*Nicely*

You may have already laid out a financial plan for the future with your daughter. Feel free to do the same with the man who wants to marry her. Run down the list of life expenses with him: housing, food, transportation, utilities, loans. Since he came to you to ask for your permission, you're within your rights to withhold that permission until you're 100 percent sure that he can support your daughter after the wedding. That's part of the conversation.

There's a fine line, though, between making this

inquiry and implying that he has a really crappy job and that he'll never amount to much. Some fathers cross that line without even realizing it. Assuming you don't want to alienate this man from the get-go, tread lightly here. Making him feel worthless simply because he isn't at the comfortable stage of life you're at right now isn't helpful; it's just mean.

 ALERT!

Remember what it's like to be young and unsure of the future and scared to death of your future father-in-law and what he might say to you. Though this guy has the very best of intentions, he doesn't have your accumulated years of life experience—don't expect him to act like he does.

You Don't Approve?

Most fathers will find themselves having this conversation with a young man they've known for some time, and they will, in fact, have been expecting to have this talk sooner or later. But what happens if you're hit with the question out of the blue and you honestly think it's a mistake for this young man and your daughter to get married?

That depends on you—and on your reasoning. If you don't like the way he dresses, that's not a good enough reason to withhold your blessing. If he's a criminal, on the other hand, you have carte blanche to speak now instead of forever holding your peace.

In the end, though, you have to realize that your daughter is an adult, and if she wants to marry him, she will. You can't lock her in her room until he just disappears one day. If you come right out and tell this man that you think he's not ready for this commitment, or that he's completely wrong for your little girl, you run the risk of being the bad guy for as long as you *all* shall live.

 FACT

The way you handle your disapproval of the engagement will affect your relationship with your daughter for many moons, so choose your words *very* carefully.

Does this mean you have to give your blessing no matter what the circumstances? No. Just keep in mind that there are different ways to *not* give your blessing— you can rant and rave and throw the guy out of the house, or you can be calm and diplomatic and discuss the possibility of waiting a year or two before he and your daughter take the trip down the aisle, with the hope that either the things that you're so concerned about improve or the relationship completely falls apart by that time.

He Never Asked?!

You've been waiting for your daughter's boyfriend to come to you and ask for her hand in marriage. You've been patient. You have a little mental list of your questions and concerns to address with the young man when the time comes . . . and then the two of them walk through the door to announce their engagement! Well, they can't be engaged if you didn't give them the green light, and now you never will, you've decided. So *there*.

QUESTION?

If he didn't come to me first, can I still sit down and discuss matters with him?
Just because you two didn't have a chat before he popped the question doesn't mean that he's completely off the hook. If you have some valid concerns about where he's headed in the future, take the time to address them.

Hang on. Your nose might be out of joint, but there's nothing malicious afoot. Men are less likely to follow tradition without some sort of prodding. If this young man never received any guidance in this area (from his parents, his brothers, or his friends) and especially if your daughter never raised the issue with him, he may well have simply overlooked this step. It isn't a reflection of his feelings for you (he doesn't think that your opinion is worthless, in other words). He just hasn't been schooled in engagement etiquette.

Try not to make this about *your* hurt feelings. When your daughter is showing off her engagement ring for the first time, don't make a big stink about the fact that no one asked you how *you* felt about this. Let them have this time for themselves. They'll still be engaged a few weeks from now, and that's when you can bring up the important matters of how they're going to support themselves and when they plan on saying "I do." Be a good guy and hold your tongue for just a little while.

Passing the Torch

Fathers around the globe (at least in countries where marriages aren't arranged) go through the torture of being traded in by their daughters for True Love. It's not easy to raise a little girl and have her think you hung the moon, only to see all that admiration—and more—recycled and given to a *new* guy at some point. Sometimes it's difficult to separate your feelings of sadness at this new phase of life from any actual feelings of dislike you might have for your daughter's potential groom. (Do you simply resent his presence, or is he really a rat?) However, with the right attitude you can gracefully handle your move from number one man in your daughter's life to a close second.

Accept It

Sad as it may be to watch your little girl suddenly hang on this young man's every word (the way she used to listen to you), it's only natural. You knew she would leave the house one day, and you probably knew that it would be to marry some guy. The time has come. Instead of focusing on how quickly she grew up (and by extension, how old you're feeling), take a step outside of the situation and take inventory: Isn't it great that she found someone that she wants to grow old with? Isn't it better that she's happy because of this man instead of being lonely and sad?

 FACT

> Any attention you call to yourself by lamenting the passing of her childhood (and her affection for you) is going to be met with harsh stares from your wife or other children, who will recognize your complaints for what they really are: the preamble to an old-fashioned pity party.

Some dads have absolutely no problem letting go of their position in their daughter's lives (this is particularly true of fathers who have left the bulk of the child-raising to their wives). They're able to see this transition as nature taking its course. For other dads (especially those who have made every effort to be a central part of their daughters' lives), this can be an absolutely heartbreaking experience—made more difficult by the fact that no one will want to acknowledge your feelings except to tell you that you're being self-centered and that you need to get over it.

Harsh words? Yes. True words? Sorry, but yes. The focus at this time is on your daughter and whether she's doing the right thing for herself. Is she happy? Is the young man in question going to make a good husband? These are the things that really matter.

Encourage It

"Yeah, right," you're thinking, "I'm going to encourage my daughter to knock me down a peg in her life. *Sure* I am."

Well, consider this: If you encourage her dependence on you and your opinion, she's not connecting with her fiancé on certain issues—in fact, she may not be connecting with him on any issues if her first thought on any big topic is always, "I wonder what Dad would say about this?" This might seem like a fine and dandy set-up to you, and it may well be keeping the peace, as far as you're concerned (hey, the boyfriend doesn't seem to mind, and you don't have to be resentful of the guy for taking your place). However, in the long run, it's a sure bet that this little arrangement is going to cause problems. Though your daughter's heart may be in the right place (or maybe she truly *hasn't* ever made a move without consulting you), in the end, this is a recipe for newlywed disaster.

So are you supposed to withhold your help and life experience from her if she asks for advice? No. Of course not. She's your baby; you'll always help her if she asks. Just be careful not to get in the middle of decisions that should be made by her and her new husband. For example, if she comes to you asking for a loan so that she can buy a new car, sit down with both of them and discuss the terms of the loan and whether both of them are in on this. The last thing you want to do is to make her husband feel as though he can't provide her with the kind of life that you and she both feel she deserves.

 ALERT!

No husband wants to feel as though he's playing second fiddle to the decisions his father-in-law is making. (If *your* wife had run to her own dad for advice on every decision that concerned your marriage while simultaneously blocking out *your* opinion, you would have been a tad bit annoyed, right?)

The best thing you can do for your daughter and her new marriage is to gracefully take a step back, away from the center of her life. There is no competition for her affections. They're completely different types of love—apples and oranges. But her relationship with her husband *has* to come first if the marriage is going to last. It's that simple.

Get to Know Him

Men are generally less apt to make an effort to socialize with a brand new person on the family scene. Many males figure that if a new guy has any redeeming qualities, they'll come out eventually, over the course of family dinners, the wedding season, and various other occasions where the opportunity to chat will present itself naturally. This may be true enough—except in a situation where there is no opportunity for family dinners, or the wedding is being planned several states away. How are you going to get to know this guy before he starts calling you Dad?

Get Outdoors

If either of you has a penchant for the outdoors, work with it. Men tend to bond quickly and easily over activities they share a common interest in. If you both enjoy fishing, take him out in the boat while he's visiting. If you're both avid hikers, hit the trails for an afternoon of climbing together.

Be sensitive to his likes and dislikes, as well as his abilities. If you're a tennis pro, for example, you wouldn't want to invite your nonathletic future son-in-law to join you on the courts. He'll take that as an invitation for you to humiliate him, and the end result will be anything but pleasant. In fact, such an unfortunate incident might become a reference point for years to come. (Imagine him saying to your daughter, "You want me to spend a weekend with your parents? Don't you remember the Tennis Match? My ego is still bruised!")

ESSENTIAL

> It's important for men to establish a feeling of trust (the reason why men who play well together can often bypass small talk and get right to the meat of things), but it's *as* important for each man to maintain a feeling of competency, no matter what the situation.

Side by Side

Don't be afraid to ask your daughter's fiancé for a little help with some of your larger chores. Unlike a sporting contest, this is an area where you can teach him a thing or two without threatening his manliness (after all, if he's never owned his own house, there's no good reason why he *should* know all about copper versus PVC piping—but this is the perfect time for him to learn). This will give you an opportunity to reap the benefits of tackling a big project together *and* promote a sense of respect—as long as the two of you can work together without cursing at one another.

If you're going to assume the role of teacher in order to get to know your future son-in-law, remember that the most effective teachers actually teach. They don't get frustrated by inquiries, they don't grab the wrench out the student's hand and say, "Oh, let me do it! You'll never get it right!" and, most importantly, they have realistic expectations.

ALERT!

Your goal here is to get to know this man your daughter intends to marry—not to browbeat him into becoming a master roofer in one weekend. That may be a nice byproduct of the encounter, but it's not the real point. Understand that before you break out the power tools.

Getting to Know *You*

Chances are, this young man will be a little nervous at the prospect of spending time alone with you—at first, anyway, until he comes to understand all the nuances of your personality. (A frown doesn't always mean you're angry, and a smile might mean that you're thinking up some dastardly deed.) Most young men who are put in the position of having a little one-on-one time with their future fathers-in-law are going to feel some pressure about making a good impression. It doesn't matter how long you've known this guy; the game has completely changed now that he has announced his intentions to marry your daughter. He's under an entirely different kind of scrutiny now, and he knows it— or he should.

Men are generally less concerned about what other men may be thinking (as compared to women, who tend to analyze the thoughts and actions of others).

However, because this man wants to make a good impression on you, he might be trying to read your mind while the two of you are getting to know each other. This is a scary thought in itself, something that's bound to end badly . . . so you should be aware of the possibility.

Don't Come On Too Strong

You want to avoid scaring this man to death, so if you know you have a very strong personality and your daughter is begging you to scale it back for a day or two, consider granting this request, at least during your initial outings with her fiancé. He's going to be an official member of the family soon, and while *you* are the head of that family, that doesn't give you the right to intimidate new members.

 FACT

Remember, he doesn't really have to prove that he can stand up to a bullying from you—he's going to marry your daughter no matter how well the two of you get along. If you want to maintain a close relationship with your daughter, it's in your best interest to find a way to get along with her future husband.

Some fathers feel as though their new sons-in-law should be able to take a little ribbing (or even some out-and-out intimidation), but truthfully, that depends on the personalities in question as well as on how you'd like your relationship with this man to proceed. If your daughter's fiancé has a strong personality of his own, he might just come out of his corner swinging back at your barbs, for example, which could be a setup for long-term disaster.

Every Son-in-Law Is Special (Really)

Everyone is special; everyone has something to offer, if you give him a chance. Haven't you been telling your kids this since they were old enough to understand what it means? Time to get back to the basics of human relationships: While you're getting to know your new son-in-law, don't draw comparisons to anyone else, especially if you already have one son-in-law who is, in your mind, the perfect addition to the family. Not fair.

Judgment Dad

Your daughter has brought home her fiancé, who is into some kind of incoherent music, who looks tired all the time (even though he apparently sleeps twenty hours a day), and whom, quite frankly, you think you might have seen on that FBI Web site you check all the time for just this very purpose. (Finally, this little hobby that your wife has called *obsessive* has paid off!) On top of that, he can't seem to make conversation to save his life—so what are you supposed to think? You're doing the work; he's supposed to meet you halfway, and he refuses. So you have every right to hate him.

No, no, no. You don't.

Put yourself in rewind mode. *Everyone has something special to offer*—even this guy who seems to have no redeeming qualities. So he's not into chitchat. There are worse qualities in a son-in-law. In fact, you may come to appreciate his disdain for small talk one day when he's visiting and *you* don't feel like talking to anyone.

 ESSENTIAL

Do whatever you need to in order to have an open mind and give him a fair chance before you write him off. The two of you will be bumping into each other for a long, long time, and if you can make the relationship palatable to both of you, you won't have to dread family gatherings.

No Comparison

In addition to the fact that your daughter intends to marry a slacker, your *other* daughter is already married—to an intelligent, well-spoken, well-connected, successful man. In fact, he's you, just thirty years younger (no wonder you dig this guy so much). He's the ideal son-in-law; why can't your bum-loving daughter see that she should be marrying someone more like him?

Oh, Dad. You know you should never compare kids; the same goes for the mates they choose. Hopefully, you were not the kind of dad who always asked your younger daughter why she couldn't be more like her older sister—and if you were, your younger daughter might be proving her point right now. She's not like her older sister; and she has no intention of marrying a carbon copy of your favorite son-in-law. That's something you'll have to let go of, and the sooner, the better.

 FACT

No one likes to have their shortcomings (real or imagined) pointed out to them. When you get into the bad habit of not only listing someone's faults, but of also contrasting them to someone else's amazing abilities, you come off not looking so great.

If you're feeling compelled to expose your future son-in-law's weak points, ask yourself why. Unless you can come up with some cold, hard facts (such as a rap sheet showing this man's history of defrauding young women out of their life's savings), you must stop. You're not going to win anyone over to your side, and the marriage is going to happen whether or not you decide to accept this new son-in-law.

Play Fair

Above all, give the new guy a fair chance to settle into the family and get comfortable with everyone before you start making judgments about his personality. You could possibly be right (sometimes father really does know best): He might be everything you think he is (or is not). But just like it's not fair to make a snap judgment about someone you meet in the business world, it's not fair—or prudent—to make the same kind of assessment of a young man you don't know.

You might just find out that his silence is due to shyness; you might also find out that the reason he slept the entire weekend at your house was because he had worked eighty hours the previous week and didn't want to cancel his trip because your daughter was looking forward to it. And maybe you'll find that his music is really quite good (or, at least, it's not *bad*).

Maybe He's *Not* That Bad

Parents who come down too hard on their kids' future mates are sometimes put in an awkward position in the future when the mate's true colors start shining and everyone realizes that he's actually a pretty good guy. You'll either have to keep up the pretense of not liking him or you'll have to apologize for your behavior— or you'll have to pretend as though you never hated him. None of these are great options, and your life will be *much* easier if you reserve your final judgment until you really get to know him.

Let Him In

Poor Fiancé. He has a hard row to hoe here, coming into an established family, trying to assess who's for him and who might not be, and all the while desperately trying to make a good impression on everyone so that your daughter will still love him when they leave your home. After all, if he can't fit into her family, will she still want him? Will she come to see him in a different light if he's the only one who can't keep up with the dinner conversation?

Try to remember what it's like to be the outsider. You went through the same thing with your wife's family at some point; how did that work out? Were they rotten to you, establishing a tradition of you avoiding her relatives at all costs? Or did they welcome you and accept you better than your own family ever did, thus instantly doubling the number of people that you consider kin?

You might feel as though nature should just take its course. If the boy fits in, he fits in, and if he doesn't . . . you can't force it. That's true to some extent, but there are ways that you can help ease his transition:

Avoid overwhelming him. Don't try to introduce him to too many family members at once. He's trying to get to know the immediate family right now; keep it simple.

Prepare yourself with a little knowledge of his interests and his line of work. If he works for a power company and you know nothing about it, educate yourself so that you can have a meaningful conversation.

No inside jokes at the dinner table. Even if your

family relies mightily on little sound bytes in order to sum up certain life events, inside jokes are *designed* to keep some people in the loop and others out.

Keep a positive attitude. Be prepared to give him the benefit of the doubt for a while. If six months pass and you're getting nowhere with this man, then you're free to make a negative judgment. For now, cut him some slack.

If you've done everything you can possibly think of and the relationship still doesn't get off on the right foot, at least you'll know that you gave it every chance. People *are* different; you might not ever see eye-to-eye with him, but you don't want to assume that from the moment you meet him. Give yourself—and him—plenty of time and opportunities to accept each other, and your relationship will be as good as it can be.

Chapter 3

The Wedding Season

"Oh come *on*," you're thinking, "What does the father of the bride have to do, anyway?" You're just supposed to put on the monkey suit, walk her down the aisle, and hand her off to the new guy, right? Not quite. Your family might expect you to be much more involved—and you may *want* to be. This chapter will walk you through some of your financial responsibilities (more on this in Chapter 4), as well as some lesser-known obligations.

Dad in Action

Game on! As soon as the ring hits your daughter's finger, she'll be awash in bridal magazines, bridal books, bridal planners, and dreams of the perfect wedding. You will stand by and wait for the anvil to hit you on the head, so to speak—that's when you'll find out what she's thinking and how it relates to your life. Get ready, get set . . .

Money, Honey

Fathers with little girls inevitably make jokes about someday paying for their weddings. When it happens, it's suddenly not so funny anymore (at least not to you). Unfortunately, if you ask anyone what your responsibilities regarding the wedding are, you're likely to hear something to the effect of, "Sign the checks and get out of the way."

 QUESTION

What will I be paying for?
The bride's family traditionally pays for the bulk of the wedding, including the bride's dress (no small purchase), most of the flowers, the ceremony expenses, the reception, the invitations, the photographer and videographer, the cake . . .

This is a good time to point out that while these expenses are *traditionally* your responsibility, tradition is hardly what it used to be. These days, more and more couples are paying for their own weddings or are at least contributing to them, which lessens the burden on your checking account quite considerably. The groom's family might also pitch in. How will you know, then, what the heck you're going to end up shelling out for? Sorry to say, but you may just have to talk to them about it.

Communicate with the Family

Dads are sometimes reluctant to communicate with anyone, let alone with a groom or the groom's family—but if you're going to be in the know on the matter of wedding finances, you're going to have to start talking to these people. If your wife is the one who is better at handling these things, that's fine—but you'll need to communicate with her.

Unless you don't want to know one single thing about the wedding, you need to prepare yourself for these conversations. First off, you're going to want to discuss the wedding with your daughter for many reasons, the biggest one being financial. If she's thinking of recreating the latest royal wedding on your dime, and meanwhile your checking account contains, literally, just *several* dimes, it's best to get that out in the open right away. It may also be best to have your daughter or her fiancé bring up the money subject with the in-laws first, too—see Chapter 4 for more on these delicate negotiations.

FACT

Planning the wedding is a delicate balancing act between what your daughter wants and what you want for her (or what you can reasonably afford). If you can't afford the 500 guests, say so, *pronto*. She might be as happy with a smaller wedding with the greatest band in town.

Stay on the Same Page

Here's where this topic segues into a chat about the emotional instability of brides: Brides can be happy one minute, weepy the next, and you never see the mood change coming. Though you hate to crush her fantasies and send her into a temporary emotional meltdown, you need to bring her down to reality—the sooner, the better. If she wants the royal treatment on her wedding day, she'll have to come up with some of that money on her own. Sure, there will be tears, but it will be *much* worse if you keep quiet until after she's already looked at reception halls fit for a queen.

For this reason, it's important for you to communicate the financial realities to your wife, as well, especially if she's going to do most of the planning with your daughter. You wouldn't want her to mistakenly offer your daughter choices that are way out of your price range, only to have to rescind the offers later.

Stand Your Ground

If you plan on being the least little bit involved in any of the decision-making, your wedding responsibilities won't end with the opening of the vault and the signing of blank checks. Educate yourself beforehand and be prepared to be firm if you're going to be visiting wedding vendors with the bride. Know what a wedding cake should cost, for example, and what it shouldn't. Be aware of the different choices for the reception meal and which are the most expensive options. (All of this will be covered in greater detail in Chapter 4.)

 ESSENTIAL

Be as firm with wedding vendors as you would be in any other business transaction. If you're shown something that's roughly double the price you've laid on the table, ask for something in your price range.

Fathers of the bride are sometimes regarded as mere accessories—the daughter knows what she wants, and her father is going to pay for it. That's just how it works, as far as some of these vendors are concerned, and some of them might actually try to use that reasoning with you in the presence of your daughter, who, you'll remember, is on emotionally shaky ground right now. Make sure your daughter knows what you're willing and able to pay *before* you enter the caterer's (or the photographer's, or the florist's) office.

If the vendor in question is just not willing to work with you on your terms, end the meeting right then and there and go elsewhere. Fortunately for you, the wedding industry is huge, and there's always someone else who will be more than happy to work with your budget and snag your business.

Be Realistic

It's important for you to know how much certain aspects of planning a wedding cost; not only to protect yourself from getting ripped off, but also so you'll know a fair price when you hear it. Be sure you educate yourself on the costs of a wedding in your particular region of the country. Be aware that in large cities, weddings tend to be much more expensive than those out in the country. Before you give the green light to any particular reception hall or florist, shop around and find out for yourself what the current prices in your area are.

 ALERT!

Don't take a caterer's word for it that no one can feed your guests for less than $120 a head—it takes a relatively short amount of time to place and field calls from competitors.

Weddings are expensive, and if your daughter wants the traditional big wedding, it will cost you thousands of dollars (at an absolute minimum). If a florist is quoting you prices for the ceremony floral arrangements, you shouldn't expect each huge basket to cost less than $25. Such expectations are completely unrealistic, and no one will *ever* be able to give you flowers for that price, unless they're going to pick some weeds and throw them in a wine bottle vase—which is probably not the look your daughter is going for.

To do proper research, you'll need to ask for literature (that is, written prices), and you'll need to know whether prices are subject to change. After you've nailed down the real prices, you can start comparing and contrasting services.

Help for Out-of-Town Guests

Because you'll likely be inviting out-of-town guests to a large wedding, you may want to make sure that their needs are taken care of—after all, they're shelling out a considerable amount of cash to attend this event; they'll appreciate knowing that you're concerned about their well-being. Consider finding and reserving a block of rooms at a nearby hotel. Some hotels will offer a discounted price for reserving multiple rooms.

Include a map of the area in the invitations that are being sent to nonlocals, a list of things to do between the ceremony and reception (or during any downtime), and explicit directions from the hotel to the ceremony and reception sites.

 ESSENTIAL

If you do reserve a block of rooms for out-of-towners, make sure the hotel is clean enough for the nit-pickiest Jane, and not above the average Joe's means. You'll be hunted down at the reception if you put your guests in a seedy motel.

Keep in mind that some people have no sense of direction. (It doesn't matter if they're blood relatives of yours, and you've given yourself the nickname of The Human Compass.) In addition to sending guests north or west on a certain route, include some land-marks so that even the most hopeless navigators will know that they're headed in the right—or wrong—direction.

What Those Wedding Terms Mean to You

If you find yourself in the midst of a wedding planning maelstrom, you might start hearing certain phrases being used over and over by your daughter and wife. This section will take you through some modern wedding terms so that you can react with your usual intelligence if and when you hear them (instead of giving the speaker a blank stare and a response that is apropos of absolutely nothing).

Destination Weddings

The term "destination wedding" refers to a wedding that takes place at a far-off location, usually at some sort of resort that specializes in these events, but a destination wedding can really be anywhere. The only limit is the earth's gravitational pull.

 FACT

> The way you see it, unless your daughter is getting married in the living room, every wedding is a destination wedding—you'll get in the limo and ride to the destination, right? Not quite.

So your daughter wants this type of wedding—what does this mean to you? It means that the wedding will probably be smaller, for one thing, because the average guest won't be willing to take a whole lot of vacation time and pony up the big bucks to fly to Aruba to catch the sunset vows. For another thing, it means that you'll probably be spending quite a bit of time (*days*) before the ceremony with the groom's family. Chapter 7 covers destination weddings in detail; for now, if you're hearing this term being thrown around, prepare yourself for takeoff.

The Parties

The happy couple will be feted and feted (and *feted*) once their engagement is official. There will be parties specifically honoring the bride, parties specifically honoring the groom, and parties to recognize them as a twosome. Which party is which?

The Engagement Party

Engagement parties are usually the first events to pop up after an engagement has been announced. Gifts are not typically given at this party, it's just a chance to officially announce and celebrate the upcoming wedding.

 QUESTION

When should an engagement party be held?
Somewhere between six and eight months prior to the wedding. You want to avoid hosting it too far in advance, and you don't want to try to fit it in too close to the ceremony, when other parties will fill the bride's and groom's calendars.

While tradition states that the bride's family has the option of hosting the *first* engagement party (yes, there can be more than one), this is not an obligation on your part, especially not in this day and age. Your daughter's friends may take over the hosting duties, or the groom's family might haul out their good china for this event—or the bride and groom might choose to honor themselves. If you are planning an engagement party, make your intentions known as early as possible to ward off parties in quadruplicate.

The Bridal Shower

The bride's shower takes place somewhere in the vicinity of one to three months before the wedding. She will be inundated with gifts (from her registry, which is covered in the next section) at this gathering. The bridesmaids are supposed to get together and host this event; if they're not completely on the ball, your wife or another relative may take over.

Bridal showers are usually just for the ladies (they will have a lovely lunch and play shower games); however, it's not unusual these days for the engaged couple to have a combined shower. It may sound silly, but if you think about it, some of the most expensive items for the home (power tools, electronics) are not things that women typically give to a bride.

So, if you're invited to a shower for the bride and the groom, stifle your objections, and grab him a nice mitering saw (or a cordless drill, or a ratchet set, or a satellite dish . . .).

The Rehearsal Dinner

You'll also be expected to attend the rehearsal, the

big run-through of the ceremony, and the rehearsal dinner, which follows. Everyone who plays a part in the wedding needs to be at the rehearsal (yes, you know how to walk down the aisle—but do you know how slowly you need to walk? Do you know where to wait for your cue to begin that march?), and usually, all the players will sit down to a meal of some sort afterward.

 FACT

The rehearsal dinner is traditionally the domain of the groom's family . . . but with tradition having fallen by the wayside in recent years, you may be called into service to help with this event.

Chapter 5 contains more information on your expected behavior at all of these parties.

Unbridled Bachelors

You know what goes on at bachelor parties. Booze, babes, and . . . well, booze and babes, mostly. Should you attend your future son-in-law's bachelor party? Ask yourself these questions, and then decide for yourself:

Do you like this guy a lot? If you saw him reeling from extreme drunkenness, would it destroy your image of him forever?

How tolerant are you of wild behavior? Many bachelor parties quickly escalate into gatherings that would make even a fairly liberal father of the bride blush.

Do you *want* to go? Maybe this is right up your alley, and you can't wait to get a little crazy with the groom and his friends and family. Have at it, Dad.

If you're really leery about attending the bachelor party, don't go. Your presence is not required there. Your relationship with the groom has been established by this point, and your attending (or not attending) this gathering isn't going to make or break your affinity for one another. See Chapter 11 for more information on making your decision, and what to expect if you do decide to go.

The Registry

In truth, the registry will affect your life very little. You should know what the heck it is, though, just in case your sister or your aunt asks where your daughter has registered for her shower or wedding gifts.

Prior to her bridal shower, your daughter (and her fiancé) will choose several stores of their liking and will sign on to have their wish-list items made available to guests of the shower and wedding. How? Most larger stores will simply hand the bride and groom a hand-held scanner; the scanner's little brain registers the bar-codes of the couple's must-have items (pots and pans, linens, dishes, silverware, small appliances—the works), which will then be downloaded into the store's computer system.

Depending on the store in question, it may also be possible for the bride and groom to register online, which gives them all the time in the world to pick and choose the right set of hand towels and washcloths. Smaller shops and boutiques may give the bride and groom a preprinted computer list of available items, which the bride and groom will physically check off or fill in (such hard work!), and a clerk will enter the list into the store's computer.

 ALERT!

Telling a potential gift giver, "Oh, they don't really need anything," is just wrong—on so many levels. For starters, it's not true; and for another thing, registries, believe it or not, usually make things easier on gift givers, who won't need to conjure up their own ideas for the perfect present.

When the shower or wedding guests come into the store, they can access the registry at the store computer and purchase the housewares the soon-to-be-newlyweds have chosen. Meanwhile, the engaged couple crosses their collective fingers, hoping that they get the things they really want (the plasma TV), while simultaneously accepting the fact that they will probably get the things that they need (the blender).

This is how the newlyweds' home will be stocked with goodies, which is why it's important for you to be able to relay the pertinent info to inquiring relatives. Don't blow this one shot at unbridled avarice for the kids.

She Wants a Wedding Consultant?

Though you have no idea what a wedding consultant might be, those women in your family sure seem to think you need one. You're pretty sure it's out of your area of concern; you have no idea at this point that hiring this consultant is going to be a fairly costly venture, although she will probably turn out to be worth every single penny.

What Is a Wedding Consultant?

The terms "wedding consultant" and "wedding planner" are basically the same thing (or, more correctly, they describe people who do the same job) and are used interchangeably. These party-planning wizards typically charge a percentage (10 to 15 percent) of the total cost of the wedding, if they're providing a full service. What do planners do? As much or as little as the bride and groom want from them.

Is It Worth It?

Most brides and grooms are looking for a planner to meet them in the middle—if, for example, your daughter works full-time and simply doesn't have the patience or the hours to plan a huge wedding, she might be looking for some professional help. Wedding consultants are an incredible asset to busy brides, because they cut the legwork in half in some cases and eliminate it altogether in others. Experienced consultants can find their way around the wedding industry blindfolded. (They already know which vendors are overpriced, which are trustworthy, and which will cater to your daughter's specific wants and needs.) Established planners also have a relationship with vendors and may be able to cut a terrific deal for you with one or more of them.

So although you might balk at being asked to pay for someone who is doing the job you feel your daughter should be doing, keep in mind that if this woman (or man) can pull off the dream wedding and keep your daughter from falling to pieces all at the same time . . . hiring this professional will be worth it.

 ALERT!

A wedding planner should work *with* the bride and your budget—and she shouldn't be condescending. If you're getting a definite vibe from her (one that tells you that she thinks your budget stinks and she's doing you a huge favor by even considering working with your daughter), move on.

Finding the Consultant

Word of mouth is the best way to find a reputable wedding planner. Your daughter might have a recently married friend or two who worked with a certain planner and can recommend her highly—or not at all. What does one ask a wedding planner during an initial interview? Start with these questions:

- How long have you been in business?
- How many weddings do you typically take on a month?
- Can you provide us with references?
- Can you work with our budget?
- What type of services do you provide?
- Which local vendors do you typically work with?

 ESSENTIAL

You want to leave the consultant's office knowing your daughter's wedding will be given his or her full attention (unlikely if this person takes on ten weddings a month single-handedly) and that he or she can brainstorm within your means.

If you're really hoping to have the reception in a location that the planner flat out refuses to do business with, your first instinct might be to walk. After all, you're hiring this person, and you should get the wedding you want. But a reputable, highly recommended consultant might know a thing or two about the reception hall that you don't (the service is horrible, it's on the Health Department's "ick" list, etc.), and could end up saving you from making a huge mistake.

Your Opinion

You've got great ideas about this wedding. You've got so many things to say, in fact, that you've started carrying around a mini tape recorder so that you can play your sound bytes at the dinner table. Why is it that no one seems to be listening? Could it be that the women just want you to show up where and when you're told to and to otherwise keep your mouth closed? Surely no other father of the bride has had to put up with such apathy from the masses.

 FACT

> You shouldn't expect that you'll be given a second (or third, or thirtieth) opportunity to prove that you really do have good taste and great ideas if you've failed to prove this in the past—or, at the very least, you shouldn't expect that it will happen *easily*.

Good Ideas versus Bad Ones

Unfortunately, even in this day and age, many issues are divided among gender lines, and many other issues become the basis for judging someone on his or her past performances. For example, if you've always pushed party planning off on your wife, you should expect nothing different from this particular time in life: She'll plan the big wedding with your daughter, and you can simply show up, just as you've done countless times before, to play the part of the host.

Likewise, if your ideas have always been dismissed by the family as being a little nutty or a tad bit over the top, you'll be hard pressed to change those opinions now, when the biggest day of your daughter's life hangs in the balance.

If you find that you are regularly being shut out of conversations that you want in on—especially if these conversations are fraught with potential problems, and *you have the answers*—your best bet is to proceed cautiously. Demanding that everyone acknowledge your genius *right now* is not the tack to take. Think of this as a little expedition; you're putting a little bait out there and slowly bringing the naysayers over to your side. Some tips:

• Instead of talking until you're blue in the face, interject with just one or two very helpful (and well-thought-out) comments. This shows you're not trying to take over the conversation.

• When someone else speaks, listen. There's no faster way to get a reputation for being a know-it-all than by dismissing the words coming out of someone's mouth before you've even heard them.

• If someone else has a better solution to a problem, admit it. Don't hold hard and fast to your ideas simply because they're yours.

• Avoid falling into old family roles. If you've always thought your daughter is a little flighty, don't assume that all of her ideas are going to be wacky. She may have changed; it's also possible that she was never as flighty as you thought she was.

• Acknowledge that other family members, though they may be younger and less experienced in life than you, just might know a couple of things that you don't. Take the opportunity to work together, and some really fabulous solutions might pop up.

The bonus to working in this fashion is that it may just have lasting consequences on the family dynamic. You may even decide that you can all sit down and agree to disagree, without agreeing to also stop speaking to each other for a week.

Please **Speak Up!**

And then there are the fathers who are so tight-lipped on everything that their families have to beg for mere morsels of food for thought. If your daughter is pleading with you to get involved and give some opinions on her wedding, for goodness sake, do it. It's not an unmanly thing to do, and this is one of the last big events of her life that will give you an opportunity to bond with her.

If she wants your opinion on the reception hall, take a drive over there with her and check it out. If she's looking for some help planning a menu and you're renowned for choosing just the right appetizers for your own parties, share your expertise with her. Sure, she's an adult, and yes, she might very well be able to take care of these things on her own—but if she's asking you for help, she's really asking for *you*. Don't make her spell it out; get your rear in gear and throw yourself into it. When the big day comes and she leaves the reception hall on the arm of her new husband, you'll be glad that the two of you had this time together.

 ESSENTIAL

> After the big day, she's going to be a wife, and sometime after that, she may become a mother—these are huge events that take you a little further out of her life's radius. Take advantage of the time the two of you have to spend together now.

Dealing with Emotional Overdrive

As alluded to earlier in this chapter, brides are skyscrapers sitting on emotional fault lines. One crack and the whole thing comes tumbling down, and the end result . . . well, it ain't pretty. What's more, the jolts can hit the same bride time and time again over the process of planning the wedding, and what's even *more*, sometimes you'll never know what causes the shaking to commence. Events that you think might drive her to destruction (the caterer canceling or the dressmaker losing her measurements) might cause nothing more than a casual twitch or two, while things that aren't huge deals in the long run (her college roommate can't make it to her shower) will bring the wrath of her nature crashing down on everyone in sight.

 ALERT!

A bride may, at times, seem like a complete stranger—and not a very likeable stranger, at that. This behavior is caused by a bride seeking attention (read: *drama*), by pre-wedding anxiety, *and* by the fact that she's probably seen other brides acting this way and feels entitled to follow in their footsteps.

Mothers are usually quite adept at dealing with their own daughter-brides; after all, they went through it themselves, and they know what's rational and what's not (in other words, the bride's mother can get away with saying, "Oh, for the love of Pete, get over it already!" if the issue at hand is less than earth-shattering). Fathers, on the other hand, are far less likely to be given that same latitude. Since you've never walked a mile in lacy, beaded, bridal shoes (or at least not as an engaged woman, you haven't), you'll never be allowed to down-play her tears.

So what are you supposed to do? First, take a deep breath. She's acting really horrible? You might want to take a sip of that Scotch you've been saving. When you've finished your own emotional preparations, read on.

Is This My Daughter?

If your daughter has always been the emotional type, you won't be as alarmed at any wedding break-downs as you would if she's always been rock solid. You should be aware, though, that any bride is prone to losing it while she's planning her wedding, and there's really no need to worry that your *real* daughter (the one you *like*) is gone for good. With the culmi-nation of the ceremony itself, the planning-related stresses usually fade away and brides return to normal soon afterward.

 FACT

Just in case you're wondering, the answer is yes—*many* brides are incredibly self-centered, so if your daughter is acting this way, it's not at all unusual. The day she admits this behavior to you (after the wedding, of course) is the day she becomes a full-fledged adult.

If your previously even-keeled daughter is all over the map with her emotions, should you be concerned to the point of losing sleep? Probably not. Obviously, if she's completely out of control, threatening bodily harm to the baker who claims he doesn't have the counter space to make two cakes that are exact replicas of the bride and groom (he's very sorry, mind you), it's time to step in and suggest that she take a break from the planning. But if she's simply frustrated, that's understandable. With the wedding and her job and life's various responsibilities, she has a lot to deal with right now.

Be There for Her

For your part, you can offer to make phone calls or to talk with a vendor who is giving her a particularly hard time. Other than that, let her take the lead. If she wants to talk about the wedding, great. Talk about it. If she's trying desperately to talk about anything other than her nuptials, be a willing contestant in *that* game. Just make sure she knows that you don't think she's being ridiculous (something that may be difficult for you to pull off if she's a highly emotional person to begin with and you *always* tell her she's being silly) and that you are willing to listen, even if you're really ready to buy earplugs. Be kind and be patient—this is a relatively short time in life, and it *will* pass, sooner than you realize.

Bratty Bride

No, no, you're thinking—your problem goes much further than simple emotions. You're dealing with an engaged daughter who is so far out of the bounds of being merely temperamental you don't know what to call it, except for a case of Horrible Bride Syndrome (otherwise known as brattiness).

Unfortunately, this isn't all that uncommon, either. It goes along with the whole self-involved complex of being a modern-day bride. Your daughter turns on the TV to find not one, but several shows that are dedicated to following a bride (sometimes she's a celebrity; sometimes she's just a Plain Jane) as she plans what is built up (mostly by the media) to be the single most important day in a woman's life.

Not only is your daughter trying to plan something that will live up to these examples on the small screen, she's also feeling pressured into making this the only day that will ever resonate with any consequence in her mind. This is *it*, as far as she's concerned. No wonder it stopped being fun for her ages ago—this is competition and it's work.

 ESSENTIAL

Bratty brides are usually their own worst enemies, because they often find themselves alone, holding their bridal planners and calling out for help—only to realize that they've alienated everyone who at one time wanted to be of assistance.

Not that any of this excuses nasty behavior. If she's suddenly copping a nasty little attitude with you and/or her mother, you don't have to accept that. Supporting her and loving her are not synonymous with taking her verbal abuse.

Lay it on the line with this bride: Tell her you understand that she's stressed out, but that you are not willing to be in her line of fire. If she hasn't reached rock bottom yet (where her friends tell her the exact same thing), she'll probably react with more nastiness. There's nothing you can do about that except stand your ground and remove yourself from the situation. If you're paying for the wedding, don't renege on the deal, but don't give in to her tirades when she demands more money for something you never agreed to (but she just *has* to have).

Despite the arguments from the media and your daughter, you do not have to spend your entire life's savings on your daughter's wedding just to prove that you love her—if she doesn't understand that now, she will . . . someday.

General Planning Considerations

At some point, you may be asked to join in the search for the ideal reception spot or ceremony site; maybe your presence will be requested at the caterer's or wedding planner's office; perhaps your daughter will want you to sample some wedding cake with her.

Some men would rather not get involved in the planning, especially if the women in their lives (the

Mother of the Bride and the bride herself) have recently fallen victim to the insanity that sometimes affects those who eat, sleep, and dream of the perfect wedding. If you can be of assistance, do your best to lend a helping hand, even if it's in an area you know very little about (it's very easy to educate yourself in these matters), even if it's something you really don't want to do (life is full of unfortunate tasks, and this one is for a good cause, anyway).

 FACT

If you're a pretty well-connected guy, you might also be called upon to cash in some favors that are owed you by local business contacts or merchants (if you happen to do a lot of business with a local restaurateur, for example, he may be willing to cut you a deal on this wedding).

How can you make sure you're actually being helpful and not simply going through the motions?

Listen. If you've been asked to contact a caterer, don't spend your time calling florists. Someone else has that area covered.

Don't put it off. If your wife has to repeatedly ask one favor of you, she's going to blow a gasket.

Keep your mumblings to yourself—for now, at least. Yes, helping out may be a time consuming venture, but you're not being asked to do *everything*.

Just remember—this is important to your daughter, and she only gets to do this once. Let her know you're in her corner, willing to do whatever you can to make sure she has a beautiful wedding day.

Chapter 4

Fork Over the Dough, Pops

Looking at the balance in your savings account brings on a veritable storm of conflicting emotions: You were very happy with this number until your daughter announced her engagement; you're prematurely mourning the loss of this money that took you so long to sock away; and you realize, though you'd never admit it, how much you *love* your cash. Of course, you love your daughter more. Keep in mind that your losses might be considerably less than you fear if someone else is pitching in.

Traditional Expenses

The bottom line on the issue of wedding expenses is this: The bride's family has traditionally been held financially responsible for just about everything concerning the wedding, from purchasing the bride's dress to making sure that no guest goes home hungry (or sober). Meanwhile, the groom's family has typically had the privilege of attending their son's nuptials, enjoying a fabulous reception, and thanking the father of the bride for throwing such a great party. Don't curse the in-laws; they didn't write the etiquette books. Here's the lowdown on what may be expected of you:

 FACT

Bridal gowns routinely cost anywhere from several hundred (for a relatively *in*expensive dress) to several thousand dollars. The amount you end up spending will be determined by what your daughter wants and how hard she can make herself cry when you tell her to find something that costs less.

Pre-Wedding Expenses

The bride needs a dress. She wants an engagement party. Your wife will be shopping around for her own lovely frock. You may want to host the in-laws in a quiet, get-to-know-you type evening out. These are your responsibilities, and though they are few at this point, their costs will add up quickly.

It's your option to host the first engagement party for the newly engaged couple. If you have no intention of doing so even though your daughter is hinting that she'd really enjoy a pre-wedding fete, speak up. She may well have a friend or two who would love to throw this particular shindig, but who is versed enough in etiquette to know that she'd be stepping on your toes if she jumped the gun.

Ceremony Expenses

Down to business. The bride's family traditionally pays for the church (a flat fee or donation), musicians, the photographer and/or videographer, most of the flowers, any decorations to be used in the church or ceremony site, transportation, and any printed items (such as invitations and ceremony programs). Most of these items are quite costly. Take the flowers, for example. That *one* expense could run into the thousands of dollars, especially if your daughter just has to see the entire ssanctuary draped in vines and garlands. (Don't worry, though, there are ways to keep these costs down. See the section at the end of this chapter for some tips.)

The Reception

Oh, it never ends. While you just dropped a bundle on the ceremony, the amount will pale in comparison to the final bill from the reception hall. You'll be feeding and watering the well-wishers, and they don't want the cheap stuff. The entire bill for the reception usually falls into your lap. In addition to the food, you'll be paying for the musicians, the decorations, and any rented items (if you're working with a caterer, it's possible that you'll have to pay for each guest to have a plate and fork . . . and a glass . . . and a seat). You'll need to order a wedding cake, too, which won't be nearly as cheap as you think it should be.

 ESSENTIAL

Depending on the caterer or site, a buffet meal could actually cost more than a sit-down dinner. Because your guests will presumably eat all that they can, the caterer will have to provide *more* food than a sit-down meal would require. You'll also pay for attendants who will serve drinks and clear tables.

Reception Food

As far as the meal goes, you'll have several options. (Everyone who's in on this decision will have an opinion; hopefully, each of you will have honed your communication skills by this point so that a consensus can be reached.) Usually, you'll be offered a choice of a buffet or a sit-down meal. Buffets are generally less expensive; sit-down meals are perceived as being a little nicer. The benefit to the buffet is that your guests will have a wide variety of choices, while the sit-down meal's big bonus is that it offers actual service (Aunt Martha won't have to get up and serve herself). The final decision here is either financial or personal (you *love* buffets, for example, and you can't wait to get your hands on those mashed potatoes).

Reception Drinks

And then, you'll have another choice to make: open or cash bar. If it's anywhere within your means, go with the open bar. Guests really hate being invited to a party and being told when they arrive that they have to pay for their own drinks.

 FACT

You'll also pay for centerpieces and decorations at the reception. You might be able to cut costs considerably here. Instead of flowers as the focal point at the tables, your daughter might opt for floating candles set atop mirrors, for example, which will go a long way toward establishing *atmosphere*.

Another option that may be available is to only serve wine and beer, or to provide an open bar for a minimum number of hours. Very contemporary brides are opting to provide their guests with one drink—in a color that matches the wedding party. (The bridesmaids are wearing pink dresses? Think Cosmopolitans, all around.)

A champagne toast is traditional, but you may want to skip this altogether, as most of your guests will not drink an entire glass of bubbly, and you'll end up paying a lot of money for alcohol that ends up poured down the drain. A good alternative? Sparkling cider or wine. Much cheaper for you, and more enjoyable for your guests.

Not Your Problem

Ah ha! There are, believe it or not, a few things that don't fall under your name in the wedding ledger of who pays for what. The breakdown of things you may not have to give a moment's thought to:

- The rings
- Flowers (the bride's bouquet, the boutonnieres, corsages for the mothers)
- The clergy's fee
- Lodging for out-of-town guests
- Rehearsal dinner

The bride and groom are responsible for paying for each other's rings; the groom and/or his family pays for some of the flowers, the clergy's fee, and the rehearsal dinner; and your guests are expected to pay for their own lodging, though you (and the in-laws) may want to arrange to have a block of rooms set aside at a mid-priced hotel nearby.

You May Get a Break

Now that you've been through the breakdown of what the father of the bride has traditionally paid for, it's time to take a little breather and point out that tradition has pretty much fallen by the wayside in the last several decades. More often than not, the engaged couple ends up paying for at least some of their own wedding, and the groom's family may end up contributing a large sum, as well. You may end up paying for a relatively small portion of this wedding, which is the good news.

 ESSENTIAL

> It may be practical to divide the reception bill equally between you, the bride and groom, and the groom's family, since the reception tends to be the most costly venture, as well as the one part of the wedding that everyone can easily have an equal hand in planning.

The potential sticking spot here is that you may have to sit down and talk wedding and money, not just with your daughter and her future husband, but with your daughter's future in-laws, as well. If they're good people, this won't hurt a bit. If they have very strong opinions or are just plain cheap (but they want their names in big, bold letters as cohosts of the event), you'll have to find a way to come to some kind of agreement with them.

Pony Up, Bride and Groom

More and more engaged couples are paying for at least some, if not most, of their own weddings these days. The big reason for this is because more couples are waiting until they're in their late twenties or early thirties to marry—which means that they've both been working for a number of years and are able to make a significant financial contribution to their own wedding. Common sense dictates that if the engaged couple has a generous amount of disposable income, they shouldn't expect the bride's parents to foot the bill for everything—unless the bride happens to come from a long line of very old money.

 FACT

Another reason brides and grooms are digging into their own pockets to cover many wedding expenses is simply because weddings are so expensive. The average wedding in this day and age costs upwards of $20,000. The more hands to lighten the load, the better.

If your daughter happens to be financially stable (she isn't getting married right out of college, for example, and she seems to have money for everything, from her little sports coupe to the best designer clothes) and she hasn't made mention of paying for a single thing related to the very expensive wedding she has her heart set on, go ahead and raise the issue. It's not a matter of your being cheap; it's a matter of being realistic. In other words, if you're about to dig into your retirement account to pay for a reception that she could cover with a couple of her paychecks, don't.

The Groom's Family

It's not uncommon for the groom's parents to chip in on the modern-day wedding. Where once they were simply invited guests at the ceremony and reception, nowadays the groom's parents may take a real interest in the planning and execution of the entire event.

Now, it may well be that the groom's parents only want to pay for a specific part of the wedding (they want to choose the band, for example, or they want to hire a specific photographer). As iong as the choices they're making are agreeable to your daughter and aren't in direct contrast to the general feel of the rest of the wedding (you're shooting for a formal affair, and they want to hire their folk-rock pals to play the reception), don't look a gift horse in the mouth. Anyone who's willing to pick up the tab for part of the wedding is trying to *help you*. Don't be angry that they won't pay for the food; be happy that they're willing to ease some of the financial strain.

How will you know whether the groom's family is planning on whipping out their collective checkbook? No, you won't ask them over dinner. It's your daughter's place to communicate with her future in-laws on this matter (or to have her fiancé initiate the negotiations). Once you have a rock-solid answer from her (such as, "Billy's parents said you should give them a call so that you guys can talk about the reception; they want to pay for part of it"), then you can take over the talks. *Until that time*, you can pretty much go on the assumption that they'll cover their traditional expenses and you'll cover yours . . . and anyplace that you end up meeting in the middle will be a bonus.

 ALERT!

What you don't want to do is plan a big wedding with the expectation that everyone will pitch in an equal amount. The groom's family may be deep in debt already. If you start throwing money around with the *assumption* that you'll be reimbursed, you may be sadly disappointed.

The Bottom Line

Go into this with a definite limit as to what *you'll* be able to spend on this wedding. Obviously, if the groom's family and the engaged couple are able to come up with some money to contribute, your daughter will be able to have a bigger, grander wedding than if you're paying for the entire thing—that just makes sense. (The more money floating around . . . well, it's just *more.*)

Don't feel pressured to break the bank because you're feeling guilty about not hiring a team of twelve white horses to draw the bride's carriage. If you need to, feel free to *gently* remind your daughter that her decision to get married implies that she is adult enough to understand the realities of life—and that sometimes means that she can't have everything she wants.

 FACT

Remember: If the groom's family is contributing significantly to the cost of the wedding, they are your cohosts. Their names will definitely appear on the invitations, and they will not be mere *guests* at the reception: They will hold court along with you.

Wheelin' and Dealin' and Budgetin'

There are so many little facets to planning a wedding, it's important to sit down as soon as things get rolling and make a list of expenses which may start affecting your life and your bank account sooner than you think. These include:

- Engagement party
- Bridal attire, accessories, hair, and makeup
- Your tux
- Transportation

- Flowers (bridesmaids', ceremony, reception)
- Photographer/videographer
- Musicians (for the ceremony and reception)
- Reception site and/or caterer
- Liquor

As noted earlier, these are your big wedding expenses, and unless you've been stashing away a little money from every paycheck since the day your daughter was born, chances are you're not going to want to pay top dollar for every single one. Which areas do you spend the most on? Is there a rule of thumb?

Ranking the Options

The best thing you can do to minimize your stress and expense is to ask your daughter to prioritize. If she really wants the best band in town, for example, then you may just have to go with the least expensive dinner option at the reception, and she may have to find a less expensive dress. If she wants a gourmet meal for her guests, then you'll have to shuffle some *other* expenses around.

Discuss where each of you is comfortable cutting back a little (perhaps you're both willing to hire the church organist for the ceremony, who will be less expensive than a string quartet) and the areas that each of you are most concerned about (if you're inviting your business associates, for example, you'll most likely want the reception to be a top-drawer affair). If the two of you are on common ground, it will make the planning infinitely easier; if you're worlds apart, then you'll at least know that you have to come to an agreement before either one of you starts signing contracts with vendors.

 FACT

> Your job in all of this is to set a limit and stick to it as closely as is humanly possible. Be responsible in your spending, and encourage your daughter to do the same. That's the best plan to stick with, no matter what size wedding you're cooking up.

Cash or Credit?

How much of this wedding are you really supposed to pay for out-of-pocket? You've always relied on credit, after all, and that's exactly how you're planning on paying for this party.

The thing about credit is this: It sometimes gets away from even the most careful spenders. Wedding costs are big expenses, and while credit might be the least painful way to take care of them (for now, anyway), maybe you *should* be feeling a little bit of the pain, rather than waiting for it to get much worse.

Here's the tricky part: In many instances, it's *advisable* to pay vendors with a credit card, so that in the event of something going wrong (the florist skips town, or the reception hall closes down), you'll have a much better chance of receiving a full refund of your deposit. Once you hand over a check, that money is as good as gone, and it's very difficult (and time-consuming and frustrating) to get it back in your hands. Your credit card company will go to bat for you if a vendor pulls a shady number, but obviously only if you've used your plastic to pay for the transaction.

 ALERT!

> Whatever you do, never pay a deposit or a bill in cash. While some small businesses don't accept credit cards, they *should* accept your check. Be very wary of any business that insists on a cash payment—something's probably not kosher with them.

The bottom line—it's wise to use your credit card to protect yourself against any dishonest vendors, but it's not wise to spend beyond your means. *Set a limit and don't go over it.* The number of people wallowing in credit card debt is astounding and can only mean one simple thing: They weren't careful with their credit. Don't make the same mistake.

Get It in Writing

Never pay anyone unless and until you have a contract in front of you that stipulates every item you're paying for and how much you're paying. Verbal agreements (the vendor's word and a handshake) are no good. Yes, the guy you're dealing with might seem as honest as the day is long. You're *still* not paying him a penny until you have a contract. If you decide to follow your instincts and trust that he'll follow through on his spoken promises at your daughter's wedding six months from now . . . you'll be sorry.

Even if you shun legalities on a daily basis, remember that a contract protects you. And if there's something contained in the contract that isn't to your liking (a section stating that the florist will make every effort to deliver at the time stated, but won't be held responsible for late deliveries, for example), don't sign it. Play hardball, get the contract you want, or take your business elsewhere.

Borrowing from Yourself

Should you refinance your house in order to pay for the wedding? That depends. Refinancing usually costs quite a bit, though the fee is usually deducted from your lump sum settlement (in other words, you're not *exactly* paying out of your own pocket). What you're left with in the end is a lower mortgage payment, a lower interest rate, a chunk of change—and less equity in your home. If you're planning on staying in your house for a number of years, refinancing may be a great option. It might just give you all the money you need to pay for this wedding. No harm, no foul, no problem.

However, if you've been thinking about putting a

"for sale" sign out front, you may want to halt the refinance train. Chances are, when you do decide to move, you'll make more on the sale of your home than you will from the refinancing.

 ALERT!

> Think *very* carefully before refinancing your home. A home is usually a person's largest asset (or liability), so you do not want to be fooling around with its value unless and until you're 100 percent sure of where you're headed—financially or physically (in the case of an impending move).

In Summary . . .

You're the only one who knows how much money you can reasonably afford to put toward your daughter's wedding. Don't be swayed into spending $10,000 more than you can swing simply because you're feeling sentimental, because you may regret that decision down the road—when you have to eat at the newlyweds' house every night for several years while you pay down that debt.

On the flip side, don't sweat the small stuff. This is your daughter's one chance to plan the wedding of her dreams (or so you hope); if something is running a little over budget, tack it up to fate and let it go. Don't spend six months brooding over the fact that the reception is going to cost you a couple of hundred dollars more than you wanted to spend. It won't be worth the energy it consumes.

Cutting Corners

So where is it appropriate to cut corners? Surely it's not appropriate to look for ways to go cheap when planning a formal wedding . . . or is it?

The trick is to cut costs without looking like you've made a huge effort to do so. You'll need to be creative— you may even want or need to have some brainstorming sessions with all of the interested parties (e.g., the bride and groom, the groom's family) during which some interesting ideas may pop up.

 ESSENTIAL

If creative friends and family members offer to help out, accept those offers! Maybe the bride has an artistic friend who would love to make the invitations as a wedding gift. Does Aunt Bev have an eye for decorating? Let her take a look at the ceremony site; her ideas might save you an arm and a leg.

Your daughter or another creative family member might decide to whip up some of the decorations herself (the bride might forego the barrage of flowers in favor of using tulle bows on the outside of the pews, for example), and the ceremony programs, at least, can be printed on your own computer. There are many Web sites that offer discount wedding invitations, too.

Saving on Flowers

Flowers can be a tough area to cut corners in. Because many churches and reception sites are quite large, the spaces really need large arrangements just to avoid looking barren. You'll need to purchase a certain minimum number of flowers, in other words, and flowers are expensive. Period.

One way to pare down the bill, though, is by finding a flower wholesaler in the area—but unless you or someone in your family has some experience arranging flowers and/or wiring them together for the bouquets, you'll want to make sure that the wholesaler offers these services, as well.

If you're thinking of ordering the wedding flowers online, be careful. These sites promise to deliver fresh flowers in time for the wedding (usually via air transport), but what happens if a storm grounds the plane carrying the bridesmaids' bouquets? Look for a contingency plan (e.g., does this wholesaler have some type of agreement with local florists?) in case disaster strikes at the last minute.

If you can't find a wholesaler you're comfortable with, get creative. For example, if your daughter is getting married in a grand cathedral, necessitating huge floral arrangements, perhaps there's another wedding scheduled for the same day—she and the other bride might split the cost of the ceremony flowers. If not, maybe your expensive flowers could be transported from the church to the reception site, thus eliminating the need for *more* flowers. And if that's not possible, why not invest in some potted plants to fill up the reception site? Those will last and provide decorations for the newlyweds' home (or yours) for years to come.

 ALERT!

> Be prepared to give and take when you're looking for ways to cut ceremony costs. Your daughter may agree to go with the cheaper floral arrangements as long as she can have the dress of her dreams.

The Reception

Now you're planning the reception. How are you going to save some money here?

First off, you'll have to eliminate the places and services that are just too expensive. This will require excellent communication skills on your part (i.e., *verbalizing* the amount of money you're willing to spend). You can't get angry with your daughter if she hands you a brochure with prices that are way too high if you haven't given her a specific dollar amount to work with.

When you find a place that's within your financial

grasp, take a good look at the services it offers. Some packages will inevitably be more expensive than others. If you really feel that an assortment of ten appetizers is ample, don't sign on for a deal that offers twenty. If you don't think that your guests need white-glove tray service (where the appetizers are offered to guests on trays, instead of the guests having to serve themselves from the buffet table), nix it. No one will be the wiser, and you'll save yourself a whole lot of moola.

Keep At It

There are plenty of other ways to cut costs. Persistence and determination are your best allies here:

• Check around the music departments at local colleges (or even high schools) for talented students to solo at the ceremony. Catch them at another wedding first to make sure they're up to the task.

• Encourage your daughter to look at *last year's* dresses. After all, wedding dress designs don't change drastically from year to year, and if she can find a final markdown in her size, she could save a bundle.

• Talk up candlelight instead of flowers at the reception. Compared to fresh flowers, candles are a bargain. Place them anywhere and everywhere the fire marshal permits inside the reception hall.

• Change the time. Morning and early afternoon receptions don't require the hosts to feed their guests dinner—which is a *huge* savings to you.

• Change the date. Peak wedding season is from April to October. Some (though not all) vendors have off-season rates.

And then there are certain things you *won't* want to do, even if it means saving some dough. For one thing, don't hire your cousin (who is renowned for his shower singing) to perform at the reception. If he's not a professional, he has no business entertaining the masses.

That maxim pretty much sums up the rest of the cost-cutting *don'ts. Don't* hire a student photographer because he'll work for practically nothing (the pictures will be worth almost as much); *don't* try to whip up dinner for 200 people at home by yourself; *don't* play bartender unless you have a liquor license; and *don't* let your nonsewing wife stitch together a wedding dress for your daughter. Yes, attempting these stunts will cost you far less money; however, these are things that are almost guaranteed to end badly.

Chapter 5

What's Expected of You When

Because you are father of the bride, others will have certain expectations of you at various times throughout the wedding season. If you've never played this role before, you may wildly disappoint these people—simply because you can't very well live up to their expectations if you have no idea what they are. Don't panic; this chapter will walk you through the behaviors the crowds (and your family) will be looking for from you at the big events.

The Engagement Party

Etiquette states that the bride's family has the option of hosting the first engagement party. *Must* you do this? No. These days, most people are eschewing tradition in favor of whatever's easiest, most practical, or least expensive. What that means to you is that the bride and groom may just decide to host a picnic-type engagement party to honor themselves, and if they do, chances are no one will think twice about the appropriateness of it.

The Host with the Most

However, if you decide you *want* to throw a party to celebrate the engaged couple's good fortune, your first step is to decide on the guest list. An engagement party can be an intimate affair with just immediate family members, or it can be a much larger event, including friends and relations from around the globe.

 FACT

Formal invitations are usually not necessary for an engagement party (the exception is a *very* formal affair). Don't hire the printer until you absolutely need to—for the wedding invites. And remember: You should only invite people who will also be invited to the wedding.

Once the guest list is settled, you'll move on to the theme you're shooting for—and keep in mind, what you're really thinking about is the overall feel of the event. Do you want a very casual evening, or a very formal afternoon party (or a casual afternoon or a formal evening affair)? Obviously, this decision will affect the final cost of the party, possibly even more than the guest list will, as you could conceivably invite ninety-five friends and relatives to your home and feed them pizza and wings, which will cost you much less than hosting thirty chums at a fancy restaurant.

 ESSENTIAL

> You have complete discretion in choosing the location of the engagement party. You can choose a very formal setting, or you can string up some Japanese lanterns and make it a down-home affair.

As the host, your duties are to be very charming and sociable (no fair pulling your trademark disappearing act), and to make sure all your guests are enjoying themselves. Mingle 'til it hurts. And remember: This is a party to *honor* the young couple, so you'll want to think of some very nice things to say about them, especially when you're asked (and you will be) how you feel about your future son-in-law.

If one of your guests asks about bringing a gift for the engaged couple, do your best to discourage it. Presents aren't expected at this get-together. Friends and relatives will have plenty of other opportunities to shower the bride and groom with presents.

Giving the Toast

The host of any formal party is usually tasked with offering up the first toast. If you're having a sit-down dinner, be prepared to speak in the moments prior to everyone digging in; if you're having a less formal affair, wait until the party gets going and most of the guests have arrived. You'll ask for everyone's attention and then offer up your kind words. Tips for giving a successful toast at any wedding-related event are included at the end of this chapter.

If You're *Not* the Host

So you're not actually sponsoring the engagement party—but you are, of course, still waving your father of the bride flag. What are your duties if you're not the one officially honoring the happy couple?

One of your most important duties is not to overstep your boundaries. Everyone knows that you're very important in the whole scheme of this wedding—but this isn't your party. If the host *asks* for your help, jump right in and give a hand; in fact, there are certain helpful things you should be doing without being asked. If the party is being held at someone's home, for example, keep an eye on the bar. Make sure it's stocked with lemons, limes, cold bottles of wine, and the like. If you can plainly see that the hostess is having a hard time serving up the hors d'oeuvres, pop your head into the kitchen and offer some assistance.

 ALERT!

> What you shouldn't be doing is giving orders—to anyone. You should be chitchatting, wearing a happy face, and telling everyone how happy you are about this engagement and upcoming wedding.

Just because you're not the official host of the party doesn't mean that you're off the speech-giving hook. You may be expected to speak, to let everyone know that you really do approve of this union, or you might really want to toast the engaged couple. Be prepared, and feel free to offer up your own toast at the appropriate moment.

Don't forget that you should dress appropriately for this party, no matter who's hosting it. As the father of the bride, you're on display. A casual party doesn't mean that you can wear your grungy cutoff shorts and arrive unshaven. For a formal affair, wear a suit; for a less formal event, think khakis and a shirt with a collar, and bring your sports coat along—just in case.

The Bachelor Party

Oh, man. Not the bachelor party. You love a good stag as much as the next guy, but are you really expected to attend your future son-in-law's farewell to singledom? You're a good sport, but this may be too much, you're thinking. How is the father of the bride supposed to get through this potentially *very* long evening?

Prepare yourself for anything. Don't expect the evening to be civilized, and if you're feeling uncomfortable, leave. You don't need to stick around so that your future son-in-law knows that you support him. Don't worry about being rude. Get yourself out of there if you feel you must.

 ESSENTIAL

> Today's bachelor parties are sometimes perceived by members of older generations as excessively wild and incredibly distasteful. And while not all of them will be nearly as bad as you think, many stags include strippers, drinking to the point of losing consciousness, gambling, profanity . . . you get the picture.

On the other hand, if you're having a good time, don't worry about feeling out of place. This is an opportunity to really cut loose with the groom and his family. Just make sure that you're not the one who ends up dancing on the bar, entertaining the partygoers. The bachelor party experience is discussed in further detail in Chapter 11.

The Rehearsal Dinner

OK, you *know* you're completely off the hook as far as the rehearsal dinner goes. You'll just put your feet up right now and think about the tasty filet mignon you're going to enjoy on the eve of your daughter's wedding, and on someone else's dime. Life is good, you're thinking.

Pop! (That's the sound of your bubble bursting.) Remember: *Traditionally*, you're not responsible for the rehearsal dinner—but if this entire wedding is turning into a very nontraditional affair, you may very well be called upon to help plan this event.

Are You Rehearsing *Eating?*

The rehearsal dinner follows the rehearsal of the wedding ceremony and is usually held either the night before the wedding or sometime within the week preceding it. The entire wedding party will arrive at the ceremony site and run through the service. You will need to arrive on time and in the right frame of mind. You may not enjoy taking directions from your minister, but on this occasion, it's really important for you to follow his advice. He does this week after week. He knows the drill.

You'll stand at the back of the church (or the banquet hall, or wherever the ceremony is taking place) and wait patiently with your daughter as each of the bridesmaids walks down the aisle in her street clothes. You'll wait for your cue (a break in the music, or when the maid of honor reaches a certain point near the altar), and then it's your turn to escort your daughter down that long aisle. While it's true that all eyes will be on her, they'll be on you too, so this is the time to practice your composure.

ALERT!

Watch out for that nasty habit that shows up when you're nervous. (Don't scrunch up your nose; don't chew on your lip.) Get a handle on your game face *now*; it will be captured on film during the ceremony, and you want to look like a normal person for posterity.

Chow Time!

After the rehearsal of the ceremony, the entire wedding party (including the officiant), along with all the spouses, will gather for a relaxing meal. The groom's family is usually responsible for planning this get-together, and if your daughter's in-laws are preparing something great, good for you. The same rules apply for any party that you aren't officially hosting: Go, be charming, and enjoy yourself. Don't try to run the show, but offer assistance as needed.

But what if the groom's parents are from out of town? How are they going to pull off this party that *isn't your responsibility*?

Here's where you have to remember: All of this is for your daughter. Though you might think planning another wedding-related event will just drain the life right out of you, it won't. If the groom's family is having a really hard time planning this event from their home on the opposite coast, be as helpful as you can. A few tips:

Tread carefully. Unless you're asked to get involved or completely take over, don't. Providing opinions and brochures are far different from *telling* the groom's parents what they should and shouldn't be doing.

Get specific. If they want your help, *ask* what kind of party they want to plan. If they're looking for something on the cheap side, don't recommend the country club.

Do some of the legwork. Even with Internet access, it's not always easy to nail down a facility's ambience or its price list. If you can check a place out for them, do it.

If you do end up taking over the duties for this event, keep in mind that rehearsal dinners don't have to be fancy or complicated. You'll need food, drinks, and a location. Can you host a backyard barbecue rehearsal dinner? Yes, you can. Chances are, the groom's family will want to pitch in on the cost, especially if you're paying for almost everything else. Don't argue. Let them.

Who Invited *You?*

In addition to the members of the entire wedding party, the minister, and their respective spouses, you should also include grandparents and godparents, regardless of where they live, along with any other special relatives. Any children attendants (the flower girl, ringbearer, etc.) are also invited to the rehearsal dinner along with their parents.

 ESSENTIAL

You might also consider inviting any out-of-town guests to the rehearsal dinner. If you've ever made the trek to a wedding only to sit staring at your motel-room TV on the night before the ceremony, you know how you would have appreciated someone including you in the festivities.

The Wedding

This is your big moment to shine. This is the moment that all fathers of little girls simultaneously dread and get all giddy over. No matter what time the ceremony starts, make sure you're leaving yourself plenty of time to prepare, even if you normally dress yourself in three minutes flat (and you're currently working on whittling that time down). Your responsibilities for the big day are outlined in further detail in Chapter 12, but the following pointers will give you a general idea of what will be expected of you.

Dress Up Time

You'll pick up your rented tux from the tux shop a day or two before the ceremony. (If it's been a while since you've rented a tux, don't worry. You'll get all the info on choosing the right outfit in Chapter 6.)

If you're wearing your own tux, you should plan to have it cleaned and pressed at least two weeks prior to the big day, just in case your shirt should be misplaced or something should happen to your pants.

 ALERT!

If you're scooting over to see your tailor about some adjustments for your own tux, do it at least six weeks prior to the wedding. The man may be a miracle worker, but he only has one set of hands and a limited amount of time in any given day.

As soon as you've got the tux home, try it on. Try on all of the accessories (the bow tie, the cummerbund, the cuff links—everything) to make sure you have every little piece of the suit in your possession. Imagine dressing yourself just before the photographer arrives, only to find that your vest is missing or is the wrong color. Taking a complete inventory before the wedding day is a must. Give yourself (and the tux shop or your dry cleaner or your tailor) plenty of time to work out any mishaps.

Keep Smiling!

You may be called "Dad," "Pops," "Hey you," "Guy," or any number of things by the photographer, and by the time you hit the reception later in the day, you will be tired of posing and smiling, but do it, anyway. Wedding albums become the focal point of clan gatherings, and you don't want to go down in family history looking as though you're truly pained by the flash of the camera.

 FACT

You may feel nervous or out of sorts, but this is the day that *all* of you worked so hard to pull together—be a good sport and do your best to make sure that everything goes as planned, and that your daughter has the wedding day of her dreams.

The photographer will likely arrive at least ninety minutes prior to the ceremony, if your daughter has signed on for pre-wedding pictures. She'll be photographed with her bridesmaids, with her mother, and with her dear old dad. After the wedding there will probably be a whole variety of family portraits for you to participate in as well.

The Reception

In comparison to the wedding ceremony, the reception is a little easier on you. You can relax a bit and hand most of the work off to the people you've hired to feed and water your guests. As the host, though, you will have a few things to take care of, so don't get *too* relaxed.

Greeting the Guests

You're the host—or at the very least, you're one of the hosts (or at the very, very least, you're the bride's father), and as such, you'll be expected to greet the guests. The bride and groom will be expected to stand in a receiving line in order to accomplish this task. You won't be—you'll be getting the party started inside the reception hall. That way, the guests will arrive, say hello to the newlyweds, and move into a party that's already in progress, instead of feeling as though they're waiting for the entire wedding party to join the festivities. Your presence gives them the green light to dig into those appetizers and to hit the bar.

Your duty here? Be charming. Say hello to everyone, even the guests you don't know. If you're a good mingler, this will be a cakewalk for you. If you're not, start practicing now. A drink or two might help you feel more at ease, but don't set up camp at the bar—no one likes to see a staggering, speech-slurring father of the bride.

Dad and Daughter Dance

You'll be expected to dance with your daughter. If she hasn't asked you about a particular song you'd like to hear, she's chosen it herself. The guests will gather round the dance floor to watch (and to see if either of you cry). In days of yore, the father-daughter dance was always a slow number—these days, of course, anything goes. If you're known for doing the Hot Chocolate or the Camel, your daughter may just choose a tune from the days of disco. Jitterbug is your thing? She may well decide on a swinging '50s song. If you're known best for your two left feet, make it clear to the bride that you're feeling a little self-conscious about the whole thing so that she can choose a song that you're comfortable with. You may also want to consider hoofing it over to a dance class to learn a step or two.

 ESSENTIAL

If she's chosen a slower song for the first dance, this is a great time for you to have a nice talk with your newly married daughter. She'll be incredibly busy, and this may be one of the only moments the two of you have "alone."

Speech! Speech!

Some people love to talk. They will talk to anyone, any-where, anytime. They will talk to themselves. They'll talk to the mirror. They talk to pets as though they're human. These same people, believe it or not, will sometimes find themselves completely tongue-tied when it comes to speaking in a public setting—such as a wed-ding-related gathering. If you'd like to give some sort of speech at your daughter's engagement party or at her reception, but you're finding yourself breaking out in a cold sweat just thinking about it, read the following pointers on how to pull this particular task off without a hitch.

"Is This Thing On?"

First, you need to decide what it is you want to say. Since this is a whole new phase of life that your daughter is entering into, you'll probably want to touch on the past and marry that vision to her future. To that end, you'll need to come up with some happy or funny memories, and you'll need to find a way to incorporate those into your good wishes in your toast.

For example, a man who has a stubbornly inde-pendent daughter might make mention of some blatant examples of how she has expressed her autonomy over the years, but will conclude the anecdote by mentioning that her new husband must be someone very special for her to want to share her life with him. A father who is toasting the marriage of his mild-mannered daughter might take a different tack: He might mention how he's cared for his little girl all these years and how happy he is that she's found a husband that he trusts to take over for him.

What you decide to say will be personal (the best speeches are); it's *how* you decide to say it that will make or break the toast.

 FACT

The order of speakers at a wedding reception, according to traditional etiquette, is as follows: best man, father of the groom, father of the bride, groom, bride, friends and relatives, maid/matron of honor, mother of the groom, mother of the bride, and anyone else not previously mentioned.

Speechmaking Pointers

If you speak to large gatherings often as part of your work, consider yourself lucky. Chances are, you've fallen into a routine of preparing yourself mentally and physically for the job, and offering a toast at your daughter's wedding will not be an anxiety-inducing event. If you never speak to more than two people at a time, however, garnering the courage to address an entire reception hall filled with friends, family, and strangers might seem like a daunting task.

Fear not, Father. You can do this. Some tips:

Start early. Think about what you want to say at least a month before the event. You'll be leaving yourself plenty of time to edit and rewrite your speech, if need be.

Write it down. You may know exactly what you're going to say, but on the off chance that nerves get the better of you when you approach the microphone, it's best to have a written reminder of the points you want to hit.

Practice. Yes, it's an old trick, but an essential one. Stand in front of the mirror and read your toast. Try not to stare at your index cards the entire time. Get your wife to listen. You'll get a feel for how the speech is coming along.

Less is more. Feel as though you're going on and on and on? You probably are. Wedding toasts should be kept to several minutes (two to three) at a maximum. Your guests will be waiting to eat, and you don't want a riot on your hands.

And remember the Golden Rule of Wedding Speeches: no negativity of any kind. Yes, everyone knows how much you love her and how hard it is to let go of your little girl. It's all right to touch on that (briefly), but keep in mind, this day isn't about you and how you're feeling. Always end on a positive note—a look to her future, which is just brimming with hopefulness and happiness.

Performing Without Backup

Of course, all of the information included in this chapter is just fine for the father of the bride who has a *mother* of the bride around to pick up the slack. What about the dad who is simply the One and Only Parent of the Bride? How do his duties vary?

Your daughter might assume that she'll have to plan the wedding by herself, because many dads are just not into the whole wedding scene. If you want to help her, speak up. She might not want to burden you with tasks that she feels you're not interested in—and *you* could mistakenly feel as though she's shutting you out because of your gender. The fact is, you can step in to help anywhere her mother would. Plan the engagement party; help her with the guest list; talk cakes and flowers with her.

 QUESTION

> **Does a single father of the bride need an escort for wedding-related events?**
> No. If there's a special someone in your life already, you'll want to include her in the festivities; if not, don't feel pressured to find someone just for these occasions. Your attendance is required at every event, though.

The dad who is forced to rely on himself during the wedding season actually has an advantage over the dads who know that they really only need to slip into their tuxes and show up. Is there any better bonding experience than planning your daughter's wedding with her? (The answer: No, there isn't.)

Obviously, there are certain areas of planning that you might feel less comfortable and capable of tackling (such as helping her choose a wedding-day hairdo or the right girdle). No one is suggesting that you have to do *everything*. But certainly, helping her interview vendors and coming up with a guest list are things that fall within your realm of expertise.

Chapter 6

Looking Good, Old Chap!

Many dads could not possibly care less about what they're wearing *or* about their general appearance. Now you're faced with looking your absolute best for your daughter's wedding and/or pre-wedding parties. You know you *can* look blindingly handsome; the question is . . . can you do it without complaining? Also at issue are your personal grooming habits. Heck, you might want to give yourself an entire overhaul. How? Read on . . .

Tuxedo Tips

Might as well jump right into the clothing issue and address the topic of the tux. Many fathers simply do not want to wear a suit that they think will feel stiff and unreasonably uncomfortable. The thing is, if your daughter is having a formal wedding, and you're included in the wedding party (you're walking her down the aisle, or you are actively being referred to as father of the bride), you're going to have to bite the bullet on this one.

One of the Guys

Every member of a formal wedding party must be dressed appropriately, and that means tuxedos for the men. Depending on what kind of tux your future son-in-law has chosen, you could end up wearing a standard-cut dinner jacket, or he may want everyone in tails, top hats, and spats. You might feel as though he's going way overboard with this, but part of your job as father of the bride is *not* to make trouble over the tux.

 ESSENTIAL

Keep in mind that not all formalwear is equal. Black-tie weddings are formal events requiring certain accessories for your tuxedo; white-tie weddings are the most formal events, and require an entirely different set of accoutrements.

If the wedding party is renting their tuxedos, all that's required of you is your physical presence for measurements about a month prior to the ceremony. You'll pick up the tux a day or two before the wedding. Don't try to squeeze this errand in on your way to the golf course; give yourself plenty of time to try on the entire suit and all the accessories. Minor adjustments can usually be made in the shop, but if someone goofed and ordered you pants that are eight inches too short, you'll be glad to know that the shop will hunt down the right size and have suitable trousers ready for you *before* you accompany your girl down the aisle.

 QUESTION

Do I really have to rent the shoes?
Unless you have a pair of patent leather shoes, yes, you should rent the shoes from the tux shop. The loafers you wear with your sharpest work suits just won't cut it in the realm of formal dress, and remember—it's the shoes that make the man.

Before you leave that shop, make sure you have everything in the garment bag, including your socks and shoes, so that you don't have to make an extra trip to retrieve them.

Buying Your Own Tux

Maybe you're thinking about buying a tuxedo for this wedding. You'd rather spend the money on a custom-fitted suit than rent one. That's well and good, as long as it matches the level of formality of the other tuxes—*and* your daughter agrees to it.

Usually the groom, the ushers, and the fathers are all expected to wear the same tuxedo at a formal wedding. The accessories may vary (the groom may wear a different vest, for example, or the fathers may wear different ties), but the jacket and pants are identical. Keep in mind that if you're the only man wearing a different tuxedo, you may stand out, not just at the wedding, but in any group photos.

If the ushers are wearing fairly standard tuxes and you're thinking of buying your own, do a little cost analysis. Renting a good tuxedo will run you close to a hundred bucks. Purchasing a good tuxedo will cost you several hundred dollars. If you know that you're going to need a tuxedo for some other formal events in the semi-near future (say, *another* daughter's wedding), it just might be more cost-effective to buy one.

Wearing Your Old Tux

Now, if you have a tuxedo up in the attic (or down in the basement) that you haven't worn since your own wedding, this is *not* the time to break it out of its dusty garment bag. For one thing, styles change, even for something as classic-looking as a tuxedo; and for another, chances are you aren't as rail thin as you were all those years ago (though in fairness, you were a little *too* thin way back then). This is not the fashion statement you want to make. Hit the tux shop and find something with a modern flair and an ample waistband.

 ALERT!

> The only way to know if your own tuxedo will blend is to compare it with the tuxes the other men will be wearing—if it's too different, you may just want to rent your formalwear for this occasion.

What Are You Wearing Now?

Dressing for the wedding itself is easy in comparison to dressing yourself for other, tuxedo-free wedding events. After all, when you're putting a rented tux on, you're just following instructions, really. You don't have to choose the clothes; you just pick them up and make them look good. But what are you supposed to wear for an engagement party? And the rehearsal? What about the bachelor party?

Engagement Party Attire

Engagement parties run the gamut from very informal to ultraformal, and obviously, your fashion choices should reflect the level of ceremony you're expecting. The trick is to nail the exact level, though, because *informal* could mean that everyone's barbecuing in a park, or it could mean a cocktail party in someone's home. You would dress differently for each of these events.

If you've been invited to an engagement party to honor your daughter and her fiancé, and you're just not sure how informal it is, ask the host. Better to make a phone call and know what you should be wearing than to show up dressed in something wildly inappropriate for the occasion. Make sure you know where you're going, what's being served, and the appropriate wear. Some guidelines:

Outdoor parties: If it's a party at someone's home or somewhere relatively casual (a park, a clambake at the beach), it's probably a fairly casual event. Khakis and a decent shirt (something with a collar) should suffice. If it's a warm-weather affair, your best shorts will do.

Cocktail parties: A little more dressy. A sports coat is a minimum expectation. The location will also dictate the formality here. A cocktail party in someone's home is less formal than a party held at the country club.

Dinner parties: Again, a sports coat is a minimum. For a dinner party held in a formal setting, you'll need the full suit and tie.

Keep in mind that it's not all that difficult to scale down an outfit that's too dressy (if you arrive at a dinner party where everyone is curiously wearing jeans and t-shirts, you can remove your jacket and tie, for example, to bring yourself down a notch or two on the fashion scale). On the other hand, it's *very* hard to dress up an ensemble that's much too casual once you've arrived at a party (*you're* the one in jeans while everyone else is wearing linen suits . . . not a lot you can do here).

Dressing for the Rehearsal and Rehearsal Dinner

This is another event where fashion choices are dictated by the location—of the rehearsal itself and the dinner that follows. Since the levels of formality of each location may be completely different (the rehearsal is in a cathedral, and the dinner is down at the corner tavern), dress to meet the requirements of the more formal location.

 ESSENTIAL

While you could theoretically walk into a 200-year-old church wearing your swim trunks, you shouldn't. Common sense dictates that you show a certain amount of decorum and respect in a sacred building (even if *you* aren't religious).

If the rehearsal is being held in a church and a much less formal dinner follows, you have a wide variety of choices. You could throw on your sports coat and trousers, or you could wear a shirt with a collar and a pair of decent pants (not jeans or shorts). If you're leaving the rehearsal to go to a fancy dinner, then you will definitely need your sports coat, dress shirt, tie, and dress pants. Again, if you're in doubt, ask your daughter or the host.

What to Wear to the Bachelor Party

Brave soul you are, daring to dive right into the bachelor party. Well, there's no reason you shouldn't, but if you choose to go, you want to blend into the crowd. (When you're standing back, watching the crowd and making sure that your future son-in-law is behaving himself, you don't want to stand out, see?)

Most bachelor parties are either held in a tavern or in someone's home. You can dress moderately well, if that's your style (khakis—the old standby—are about as elegant as you should go); you can also definitely get away with wearing jeans to most bachelor parties.

One instance where you would throw on your sports coat would be if the party is being held immediately after work and everyone else will be arriving in their business suits. But since most bachelor parties are mainly about drinking all night long and suffering for days afterward, you'll probably be looking at a weekend gathering, and your dungarees will do nicely.

The Casual Wedding

Your daughter isn't into the big wedding thing, and she's chosen to get married at City Hall. You're still going to walk her down the aisle, but you have no idea what you're going to wear. You shouldn't rent a tux for this . . . should you? Should you throw on your best pair of pants and a nice sweater? And what if she chooses to get married in the backyard? You can't really wear your shorts, can you?

 ESSENTIAL

Most "casual" weddings will require the men to wear suits, which means that your outfit is really only casual in relation to a tuxedo. Don't plan on arriving in your comfortable sweats. Very few (if any) weddings fall into the realm of being *that* relaxed.

Check In with Her

Remember, what you end up wearing to your daughter's wedding depends on how formal an event it's going to be. City hall weddings are not necessarily thirty-second, who-cares-what-you're-wearing affairs; likewise, a casual ceremony in the backyard could be very informal, or it might be a little dressier.

If your daughter is planning a less-than-formal affair, ask her what she and the groom are wearing. That's the best way to determine the formality of the event. If, for example, she's planning on wearing a rather traditional bridal gown or some sort of formal dress and her groom is wearing a suit, you'll wear a suit, too. Informal and semiformal (daytime and evening) weddings are suit-appropriate events.

Summer Weddings

A casual summer wedding may have special rules, depending on where you live, and depending on how the bride wants her wedding party to be dressed. If you reside in Texas and your daughter is planning a rather last-minute outdoor ceremony in the middle of August, she may take pity on the whole lot of you and give the green light to lighter fabrics, such as linen or cotton, instead of insisting on traditional dark suits at her ceremony.

 FACT

A good rule of thumb is that summer weddings (whether they're formal or casual) usually allow for lighter colors and lighter blends of fabric. Informal fall and winter weddings, on the other hand, usually dictate that the men be dressed in darker, heavier suits.

The Well-Groomed FOB

You see it everywhere these days: Men taking their appearances *very* seriously. They're into skin care, hair care, nail care, and plucking their eyebrows. . . . Now, maybe you come from the old school of thought, where real men leave the primping for the ladies. They're the ones who need to look good.

Of course that's just not true, and you know it. Everyone likes to look his best, if for no other reason than looking good makes you feel good about yourself. Sure, there are the rare individuals out there who eschew appearances—for themselves and for others—but everyone *else* is living in our appearance-driven society, for better or for worse.

This section will cover some of the larger areas of concern in male grooming. Promise yourself to read through the next few pages with an open mind. No one ever improved himself by being cynical, you know.

Your Hands

While it's true that women are expected to have pretty, feminine hands, and men are more likely to have hands that show how hard they work, everyone benefits from the wonders of hand lotion. Your wife will suddenly want to hold your hand, and you'll remember what it's like to have skin instead of sandpaper covering your digits. And really, moisturized hands are the least conspicuous as well as the easiest improvement one can make.

Your nails are another story. What kind of shape are they in? Are they cracked or yellow? Might there be a fungus among us?

If your nails are discolored or peeling, see your doctor. If they're just badly misshapen, get yourself a manicure. Sure, you'll feel funny at first if you've never had your nails pampered, but you might just love it once it's done. Your hands will look as though you've never put in a hard day's work, and you won't believe the difference this one little improvement will make to your state of mind.

 ALERT!

Another reason to keep those hands in good shape: Those little cracks can be entry points for bacteria and germs. You might be doing your health a favor by keeping the skin on your hands intact.

Hair Raising Issues

"Not the hair!" you're thinking. You can't understand why your wife and daughter have so many issues with your locks, because, after all, they belong to *you*. Maybe you love your hair the way it is; maybe you just aren't looking for a change. Whatever the case, if the women in your life have been after you to do something with your head, ask yourself *why* they're so adamant about it.

- Is your haircut dated? (Are you sporting long, feathered hair?)
- Does it reflect a totally different time in your life? (Are you still wearing a flattop because you

got used to it in the Army . . . and you've been
out for almost twenty years?)

- Does it need a little snip here and there? (Is it
long enough to braid?)

Now, according to the story of Samson, a man's
strength is all bound up in his hair. According to sci-
entists, however, that's just not true, and cutting your
hair will *not* drain the energy from your body.
Considering that most men wear their hair short, a
haircut is a fairly low-risk venture—it *does* grow back,
and fairly quickly. Besides, you'll probably be surprised
at how quickly you get used to a slightly new look.

 ESSENTIAL

Do you have to be one of the beautiful people
to make a good impression? No. Do you have
to make an effort to clean yourself up and
look your absolute best at your daughter's
wedding? Yes. People will expect the father of
the bride to take it up a notch for this event.

One word of warning: Try out a new look *well* in
advance of the date of the wedding. For many men,
there's a delay of at least a week or two between the
time they have their locks shorn and the time it starts
looking and feeling just right. In the case of a really

drastic change, you may need to allow more time for this transition (if for no other reason than you'll need the time to get used to your new look).

What About Those Eyebrows?

And speaking of hair issues . . . it's time to address your eyebrows. A decent barber will trim those caterpillars for you, but he probably won't shave what is known in certain circles as a unibrow (or in others as a monobrow). If you have one line of wool starting at one temple and continuing across your eyes and the bridge of your nose right on over to the other temple, you should really give some thought to weeding out some of that hair. This one little adjustment will make a world of difference to your appearance. People will know *something* about you has changed, but they won't quite know what.

 ALERT!

Check for any stray ear and/or nose hairs before you leave for any big event. While you're doing your best to charm folks, you don't want them thinking, "Whoa! Look at that thing coming out of his ear!" Another small improvement that no one will really take note of—unless you don't do it.

Some men will need an eyebrow waxing to accomplish this, and unless you know anything about waxing body hair, leave it to a professional. In fact, if you've never touched your eyebrows before, don't even try to take the tweezers to them yourself, as you could end up really regretting it in the end. Let a professional shape them for you the first time; you can handle the maintenance after that. You'll find these eyebrow magicians in many unisex hair salons and day spas.

Shaving Like a Pro

Yes, you've been shaving for years. You're good at it, and no one needs to tell you how to do it. Case closed.

Well, just for kicks, why not read through this section and see if anything jumps out at you? You know, when you do the same thing every single day for years and years (and years), it tends to become a robotic, thought-free process. When was the last time you really gave any thought at all to your shaving routine? If you could improve on it and have your skin come out looking and feeling smoother, wouldn't you? Or, perhaps you've been sporting a beard for . . . well, *forever*, and you've decided to revert back to clean-shaven skin. Treat your skin right, and you'll look like a million bucks.

For starters, electric razors are not the best choice. They can be very unkind to your skin, as they are apt to pull the hair out of your beard rather than shave it, which can lead to all sorts of irritation. If you're traveling and you need a quick shave on the road, an electric razor can be a godsend. If you're in the comfort of your own bathroom, a wet shave is the better choice.

 ALERT!

Using a foam to shave with? Ouch! The benefit to using a foam is that it lathers up nicely; the drawback is that shaving foams tend to be very drying (and therefore, irritating) to skin. A shaving cream or oil is a better choice.

Now, men are often reluctant to break out a new razor. (After all, you might argue, the one you've been using for the past three months is still working just fine.) Ideally, you should be using a razor with a very sharp edge. Shave the hair in the direction it's growing to eliminate the possibility of ingrown hairs. Take your time, especially when you're shaving your neck. Men tend to want to get this mundane task over and done with, and some of them spend the day with little pieces of toilet paper stuck to their various nicks, or razor burn lighting up their cheeks. Slow down. Take sixty extra seconds to do it right, and you won't have to suffer.

When you're done, rinse the remaining cream or oil off of your sleek, baby-smooth face with cool water and use an aftershave balm to cool irritated skin. Then take a gander in the mirror and *ooh* and *ahh* over yourself. See? Doing things a little differently isn't so bad after all.

Fightin' Weight

If you've been lugging around a few extra pounds that you've been meaning to drop, you might feel as though there's no time like the present. After all, you're going to be seeing a lot of long-lost family members and friends at all of the wedding events, and it's only natural that you'd want to look your best. Is this pure vanity? Not really. Remember: Looking good makes most people feel pretty good about themselves. When people feel self-conscious about their appearance, they might tend to be a little reserved or even standoffish in the company of seldom-seen loved ones and old chums. Conversely, when people are happy with their appearance, they're more likely to put on a happy face and actually *enjoy* mingling with folks from the past.

 FACT

People who are overweight are sometimes incredibly comfortable in their own skin, and model-thin folks are sometimes very *un*happy. There's no hard and fast rule for how you *should* look; it's how your appearance affects your state of mind that's important.

Your Strategy

So let's say you want to get in shape for those wedding pictures. How are you going to do this? You're going to stop eating for a while? Cut yourself back to a few crackers and a can of diet soda at lunch? Or are you just going to eliminate the double cheeseburger you usually order with your fast-food takeout?

When you're looking to lose some weight, remember: Slow and steady wins the race. Make some healthy adjustments to your eating regimen (starving yourself isn't healthy, and eating fast food every day isn't, either). Look to add some fruit and vegetables to your diet; cut back on the fat. Everything in moderation.

Get Moving

Being active is a key part of losing weight and keeping it off. You don't have to jump into marathon running. Just find something that literally *moves* you that you can enjoy, or at least tolerate. If you find walking three miles is boring you beyond belief, ask yourself if some music—or talk radio—would help to pass that time more quickly. If you find that one type of exercise isn't floating your boat, look for something else. Are you into team sports? Look for an adult league. You want to swim, even in the winter? Find a sports club with an indoor pool.

The right exercise fit for you *is* out there—your mission is not to throw in the towel too soon. A lot of people will say flat out, "I hate to exercise." This hardly gives a particular activity a fair chance at winning you over. If this sounds an awful lot like someone you know (someone like *you*, for instance), lose the exercise label. Think of it as simply spending thirty or forty-five minutes moving your bod.

ESSENTIAL

> You're never too old to try something new. If you've always wanted to try tennis or golf, for example, but were afraid you'd make a spectacle of yourself, take some lessons. You might discover a new passion in your life—and one that keeps you fit, to boot.

The Payoff

There'd better be a big payoff, you're thinking, 'cause you hate to exercise. (We just covered this opinion in the previous section. Adjust that attitude.)

Well, aside from looking good and feeling good about your appearance, you may just start to feel healthier. Carrying around extra weight can be a burden that you don't even recognize. Just tying your shoes can be difficult and exhausting if you're fighting for space when you bend over.

Of course, there are sometimes health risks associated with being overweight, and these can only be determined by your doctor. But if he or she has been pestering you to slim down, this might be the perfect time to do it. Not only will you look like a fab father in the wedding pictures, but you might just achieve the ultimate payoff: extending your life expectancy. Your family will thank you.

Take It Easy on Yourself

Many, many people face the struggle of slimming down, and you might be surrounded by stories of failure. ("Cousin Eddie has been trying to lose weight for twenty years, and he just can't do it!") Losing weight is a personal venture; it has nothing to do with whether your next-door neighbor has succeeded with his weight-loss goals or whether everyone in your family is heavy. This is about *you*, and you alone.

If you have a bad day (you just couldn't resist the drive-through, for example, and you went for the Mighty Combo meal instead of the salad), don't let that be the end of your quest. It happens to almost everyone, even those who have successfully lost weight.

Most importantly, remember: It takes time. You can't expect to drop thirty pounds in a month and have it stay off. It just doesn't work that way. Aim for little victories (losing a pound or two a week—that's realistic and absolutely doable for most folks) and you'll come out triumphant.

Chapter 7

Destination Weddings

Aloha! Bon voyage! Sayonara! Practicing your foreign phrases for a destination wedding is certainly wise, but do you have the slightest inkling how a destination wedding differs from one held in your hometown? What about the financial breakdown, the guest list, and all of the extra planning that goes into a traveling wedding? What are you responsible for here? For starters, get your suitcase out of the attic, and make sure to bring an open mind along on this trip.

Destinations Defined

Destination weddings are growing in popularity as more and more engaged couples are becoming enchanted with the idea of having the perfect sunset wedding on a Caribbean island, or a ceremony in the meadow of an ancestral home. (Sounds too dramatic for you? Just try to remember what it was like to be so enamored of your mate and the very idea of saying "I do.")

 ESSENTIAL

> While many destination weddings take place in and around resorts that specialize in hosting these events (which makes the planning infinitely easier), by definition, a destination wedding can take place anywhere.

If your daughter is throwing the "destination wedding" phrase around, she may be thinking of a very traditional ceremony somewhere off the map, or she may be thinking of a really offbeat and unusual wedding in a spot that's central to all of the invited guests (or any combination of these aspects). Your travel time could range from a few hours to an entire day in the air, depending on the location the bride and groom have chosen.

While centralizing the ceremony may be more convenient to some of your out-of-town guests, your in-town friends and relations may see it as incredibly inconvenient.

In other words, there's no way to predict how the destination aspect of the wedding will affect the final guest count. You may be surprised to learn that your whole family loves a good, long road trip—or that they're all afraid to travel outside of the city limits.

Where, When, and How

Any weeklong vacation involves a lot of planning, shopping around for the best rates, and, for many folks, stressing. Throw a wedding into the mix and things could break down before anyone has a chance to say "I do." Is your daughter nuts, taking one potentially stressful event and trying to plan another one around it?

Planning an Out-of-Town Event

Planning a local wedding is hard enough, you're thinking. How on earth does your daughter think she's going to successfully pull off planning the wedding of her dreams when the wedding site is hundreds of miles away—*and she's never been there*?

 FACT

The cost of hiring the on-site coordinator is often included in the price of a wedding package. The package may also include some typical wedding expenses, such as food, drinks, flowers, pictures, the wedding cake, and music.

The truth is, she may have made the planning of her wedding substantially *easier* on herself by choosing a destination wedding, especially if she has chosen a resort that caters to these types of events. Many hotels that routinely host these events have an on-site wedding coordinator who will cover all of the bases for the bride and groom.

If, on the other hand, your daughter has chosen to take her vows in a fairly unusual spot (and there isn't a coordinator on site), it may be in her best interest to hire a wedding planner based in the area. It's unwise to choose a florist or a caterer out of the phone book, sight unseen, and if there's any situation where a wedding planner is worth every penny she charges, this is it.

Back to Nature

Many couples will choose a tropical resort as the site for their wedding ceremony. The beauty of leaving their wedding in the hands of a resort that handles many, many weddings is that the ceremonies tend to go off without a hitch. They're very different from the weddings back home—you're standing near an altar on a beach, or in a chapel near the resort, surrounded by the sheer magnificence of a sunny, exotic location; of course, the officiant will most likely take care to make the ceremony as personal and as moving as the bride and groom want it to be.

The bride and groom may swing to the opposite end of the thermometer and choose a destination in the mountains. Again, Mother Nature lends a hand with the scenery, and most of the details are left to the resort.

A Wedding Cruise

Cruise ships are becoming popular sites for out-of-town weddings. Many cruise lines offer wedding planning service, or your daughter may want to call her own travel agent and let him or her do the honors. Like every other destination wedding, the price of a cruise ship wedding can vary from around $1,000 (a low, low price for a three-day cruise which includes all the basic must-haves: the officiant, pictures, accommodations for the newlyweds, plus a reception and cut-rate lodging for five or six guests) to much, much more—depending on what type of wedding the couple is looking for. A small, simple, weekend wedding celebration on board a luxury liner will obviously cost much less than a grand affair for three hundred guests. No matter the size of the wedding, guests are expected to pay their own airfare and lodging.

The couple will not take their vows at sea; the marriage is most often held in port for legal reasons.

 ESSENTIAL

Cruise ships employ huge staffs trained to carefully choreograph and execute events of all sizes, which ensures that *everything* will be taken care of with amazing speed and dexterity.

Timing Is Everything

Since travel is obviously involved in the destination wedding, the entire event will most likely be stretched out over a matter of days, or even a week or more. If you're traveling to the other side of the globe, you're going to want to give yourself a few days before the ceremony to recover from the travel; if the wedding is within driving distance, you may only need a day to get your bearings and take care of last-minute business before the wedding.

 ALERT!

There's sometimes a tradeoff, of course, for snagging cheaper rates in a tourist area: Mother Nature. Planning a wedding in an exotic location during hurricane or typhoon season might suddenly seem like a bad idea if a hurricane blows in, *or* it might seem doubly exciting.

If you're in on helping to plan the destination wedding, you should know that timing is sometimes everything—especially if you're all headed to a touristy spot. If the wedding is planned for the peak season of the chosen destination, everything will be more expensive, and the place may also be densely packed with other vacationers (and other couples vying for space at the resort's altar). In the off-season, prices will be lower and you may find that you have the entire resort to yourselves.

Bridal Booking Beware

If your daughter is considering a smallish destination wedding, you might want to do your darndest to discourage her from booking hotel rooms through an online discount travel site. For larger weddings held at a resort or hotel, she will communicate directly with the facility and will most likely be treated like a princess by the reservation staff; however, she should know that customers who book rooms through online travel sites are sometimes not treated with the same care as patrons who book through the hotel itself. These customers are also shocked to find that they have no leverage at the front desk when they complain.

If something should go wrong, she may be surprised to find that the hotel management is reluctant (or flat out refuses) to make any concessions, since she actually paid the discount Web site, and not the hotel. The ball is then in the travel Web site's court—will they refund some of her money, or won't they? (It's kind of beside the point, actually, if her wedding weekend has been ruined by the experience.) It's best to leave such important arrangements in the hands of a travel agent or to book through the hotel's own Web site or toll-free number.

All-Expenses-Paid Vacation?

The minute you heard your daughter was getting married, you started tallying up the cost in your mind—each vendor was allotted a certain amount, and you had a final monetary figure that certainly hurt a bit, but it didn't lay you out flat and in traction.

Now that your little girl has her heart set on a destination wedding, you're feeling faint. This completely obliterates your original accounting work and takes you into an entirely new realm of finances, you fear. This wedding could bankrupt you if you're expected to cover the bills for the wedding, the reception, the travel, and the accommodations. That light-headed feeling is pretty darn persistent, and you fear you may have to send your own regrets.

Get yourself a paper lunch bag and take a few deep breaths. It's not nearly as bad as you think.

Cheaper for You?

For starters, because the bride and groom have chosen to marry one another in a distant location, *they* are generally held responsible for most of the wedding costs, including the wedding package itself (including any transportation, food, drink, music, etc.), the lodging and airfare for their attendants, and their own sundry expenses (the honeymoon, for example).

Does this mean that you'll *only* pay for your own travel expenses? Possibly. But depending on any prior wedding negotiations, your financial situation, and the cost of your travel to this distant ceremony, you may want to offer the bride and groom a monetary wedding gift to help defray the cost of their destination wedding—especially if you were going to pitch in on a local ceremony. Money is money, and they could probably use it no matter where they're taking their vows.

ESSENTIAL

A big benefit of the destination wedding: The newlyweds won't have to take off during the reception to catch their honeymoon flight, because, after all, they're already there.

Speaking of Money . . .

Before you assume that this wedding will be a spending extravaganza the likes of which you've never seen, you should realize that, in many cases, hosting a destination wedding is actually *less* expensive than hosting a grand, over-the-top affair back home.

For one thing, the bride and groom often choose to invite only a small number of people—it may well be that part of the reason they've chosen a distant wedding spot is to escape the crowds. The smaller the guest list, the smaller the reception, obviously. If the couple chooses to invite only immediate family and their closest friends, the reception might just be a nice dinner in an upscale restaurant—the cost of which is miniscule in comparison to feeding the entire family, your office, and various strangers at the country club.

Following that train of thought (the one that suggests that the bride and groom are scaling the wedding down to a manageable size because they want it to be an intimate gathering), the couple may also choose to cut back on other expenses that they deem frivolous—

lots of flowers, for example, or the $3,000 wedding gown. In other words, they may have chosen a destination wedding because they have their heads on straight.

 FACT

Considering what the average wedding costs in a large metropolitan area these days, the bride and groom who have planned ahead are likely to be able to foot the bill for a destination wedding *and* their attendants' travel expenses and still come out ahead of the game.

The Guest List

While the guest list for a destination wedding is often much smaller than the guest list for a typical wedding, that's not always the case. Some couples genuinely want everyone to join them in the fun and invite everyone they can think of—family, close friends, and acquaintances alike. There's just no way to tell for sure who will be up for the journey and who won't. A ceremony that's being held hours from home might yield only immediate family who are willing to make a road trip, while a wedding in the South Pacific could attract a long list of well-wishers.

Keep in mind that most folks only have so much vacation time from their jobs, and they may not want to spend it at your daughter's wedding. Some families may have already booked their vacations elsewhere, and some may not want to shell out big bucks on a trip that they never intended to take. On the other hand, a wedding is a perfect nudge for some workaholics to take vacation time, and if the location is really interesting, you may end up with the entire guest roster ready for action.

While guests are expected to bite the bullet and cover their own expenses, you may want to assist any immediate family members (Grandma, who's on a fixed income, for example) with the cost of travel to a destination wedding.

 ALERT!

Any invited guests are expected to pay for their own travel and lodging expenses. Make sure that the guests know this before they book their flights and/or arrive at the wedding site, expecting a free ride for the entire week.

What to Expect

You're getting the picture . . . you think. A destination wedding can be anywhere and take any form. But the real point is that it's different from what most of the bride's friends are doing, and it also fosters a real sense of family because you'll all be spending a lot of time together in the days before the ceremony.

So what might your experience at the destination wedding be like once you all get there?

Playing It (Relatively) Safe

Resorts that deal with destination weddings on a regular basis know how to help the bride prepare for her wedding; the receptions are set up and ready for the guests (whether the couple is expecting eight friends and relatives or eighty), and there's someone in charge who can be taken to task if things aren't going as planned. Much like a wedding in a banquet hall in the bride's hometown, there's a certain safety in this plan.

Your role here? Show up, be good company for everyone around you, and follow your daughter's instructions.

Taking a Chance

Now, if the bride and groom are bound and determined to go where no other couple has gone before and take their vows in a *really* secluded, distant place . . . all bets are off. Chances are, the ceremony will still be beautiful and touching, but since the ease of settling the details may be a little tougher, the entire day might run less smoothly than it would at an all-inclusive resort. If the couple is running their own little reception in a park, for example, it may well turn out to be lovely, but no one should expect things to tick along like clockwork. It will most likely be less formal, but there's nothing wrong with that.

You may be called on to assist during a destination

wedding where a planner isn't involved. In fact, you may become an incredibly valuable resource—the go-to guy. You might find yourself running to the store for ice, or standing out front directing guests to the correct location—you could find yourself doing anything, really, that a planner or a banquet manager would normally take care of. Jump into your role with both feet. This could be a little stressful at times, but it's also likely to be a lot of fun.

ESSENTIAL

A destination wedding can be a stress-free event—for the bride who has handed everything off to a planner. The bride who's trying to plan a long-distance or off-the-beaten-path wedding on her own, however, could probably use some help. Make things easy on everyone and ask her well in advance of the ceremony if you can help out in some way.

Overall Advice

If you've never heard of a destination wedding, let alone attended one, the best thing you can do is to enter into it with no expectations. The destination wedding can be as traditional or as nontraditional as the couple wants it to be; it can be very formal or incredibly informal. It can be anywhere, in any season, at any time. Because this isn't your event, and you really do have to attend, all you can do is try to enjoy yourself. And remember: Just because there isn't a cathedral involved doesn't make it any less of a valid ceremony. Go with the flow on this, even if it's against your better judgment.

Getting to Know You

So, you've just realized there is a very good chance that you will be spending the days before your daughter gets married in an unfamiliar place with people who may be virtual strangers to you—the groom's family. If you're not very social to begin with, the very thought of setting up camp with these folks and making charming chitchat for days on end might inspire you to hop the wrong flight and spend your daughter's wedding week in an undisclosed location.

On the other hand, you may be the one who is a little too talkative for other people's tastes, and your daughter may be begging you to cool it before you scare off her new in-laws.

Where's the middle ground here? (And what if you simply can't stand these people?)

Unveil Yourself . . .

If you're one of those dads who likes to be alone much of the time, the very idea of being forced to spend a huge chunk of round-the-clock time with your daughter's new in-laws might seem like sheer torture.

You don't like to talk; there's really nothing anyone needs to know about you that hasn't been said a million times already; and, as far as you're concerned, people who talk a lot are nincompoops.

 ESSENTIAL

There's no use trying to pigeonhole dads into categories when it comes to socializing, because some fathers of the bride love to meet new folks and really get to know them, and others simply don't. Of course, still others fall into that gray area somewhere in between.

Fair enough. You've got your reasons for being the strong, silent type. But remember: If you come off as a surly, unfriendly guy, you're making things really difficult for your daughter, regardless of her own relationship with her future in-laws. If they love her, they're going to pity her (*unfairly*, mind you) for growing up with a dad like you (because they don't know the real you—and apparently never will, if you have your way). If, on the other hand, they aren't exactly gonzo for your little girl, your attitude isn't going to help matters; they're going to draw assumptions that the apple doesn't fall far from the tree.

How can you help? By putting on your friendliest demeanor, no matter how badly it hurts. This is one of your duties as father of the bride—think of yourself as a representative for your entire family. You are, presumably, the head of the clan—strive to make a good impression, for your daughter's sake if not for your own.

. . . Within Limits

Being friendly doesn't mean that you have to expose your innermost thoughts and secret desires to people who really don't need to know them. In fact, if your moments of brilliance are routinely met with genuine confusion from your immediate family and closest friends, you might want to keep them all to yourself while you're hanging out with the groom's family.

Likewise, if it's obvious from the start that the groom's family are ultraliberal and you toe the conservative line, think twice before arguing matters of politics—or taking a belligerent right-wing stance on any current event. Of course, there's nothing wrong with being a liberal or a conservative—that's entirely beside the point. The point is that there truly *are* certain issues that shouldn't be discussed in mixed company, because more often than not, these topics lead to polarized views and hard feelings.

If the groom's mother insists on bashing the front-runner for your political party, for example, remember that *she's* the one who's behaving badly. You don't have to be goaded into an argument simply because you don't agree with her. You're more civilized than that, *aren't* you?

Bottom line, if you find yourselves at a resort for an entire week before the wedding, socializing with the groom's family night and day, try to make the most of it, and remember that this is actually an excellent opportunity to get to know everyone. At the very least, you'll know exactly what your daughter is talking about when she talks about her new in-laws' odd habits.

 FACT

Is this book advising you to be a big phony? Only if it helps matters. Remember: You're stuck with these people for now. You can spend your time sparring, or you can try to raise the bar by leading the discussion toward neutral topics.

Planning Your Time

So you're off to spend a week or a long weekend in a very interesting location to celebrate your daughter's marriage. Will you be spending every single moment staring at her, shaking your head, and wondering where all the years have gone?

Heck, no. She'll be busy doing her last-minute wedding things (or she'll be staring dreamily at her almost-husband, wondering how she got so lucky). If you're spending more than a day or two on site, chances are you're going to have some downtime. What will you do?

Get yourself a good map—and if the place is a real tourist spot, throw in a few brochures. See what's shaking in the area. What catches your eye? Are you an adventurer, looking for a climbing expedition or a snorkeling session? Are you into culture, in need of your daily fix of art or theater? Do you simply want to relax under a tree and catch up on your sleep?

 ESSENTIAL

Don't forget that, in addition to attending your daughter's wedding, you're spending a lot of money to visit this spot—and you probably won't be back again soon. Make the most of your time and money and get a real feel for the place. You're on vacation!

Assist the wedding guests in making the most of their time, too. As father of the bride, people will expect that you can fill them in on the details, even if you know absolutely nothing. If you haven't been given the lowdown, educate yourself on the area you're staying in and become something of a touchstone for the guests. Think of it as another little duty that will set you up for Father of the Bride of the Year.

After the wedding, you may not see the bride and groom again until you're all back on your home turf—and if that's the case, roll with it. Since you've all been together in the same spot in the days leading up to the wedding, it may be strange or awkward to put the kibosh on communicating with the newlyweds—but they *are* on their honeymoon, after all, and they only get to do this once. Give them their space after the ceremony.

Hometown Receptions

Some couples (or their parents) will choose to host a reception in their hometown after the wedding. If it's very important to you (or to your wife, or to the in-laws) to host a post-wedding soiree for the newlyweds, it's a perfectly acceptable practice. Proceed as you would with a normal wedding-day reception—with a few differences, and a few caveats:

- These parties tend to lean more toward champagne and cake than toward a seven-course meal.
- Assuming the reception is not being held in the park, you should wear your best suit. Tuxes are not necessary (unless it's a black- or white-tie event).
- The couple is free to register for gifts . . . but they might want to think twice about doing so.

Gifts Are Overrated, Anyway

Here's the thing with post-wedding receptions, especially if the bride and groom opted for a destination wedding because they didn't want all of these guests at their *actual* wedding: People sometimes take great offense at being asked to celebrate a marriage that they weren't invited to attend. Now, if the entire family *was* invited and most of them simply couldn't make it, that's one thing, but if they were excluded from the get-go, you might hear a few rumblings along the lines of, "Oh, we weren't good enough to go to the wedding, but we're good enough to bring them a present!"

Or worse, you won't hear the sniping and you'll be left to deal with offended friends and relatives who feel obligated to show up at the reception, but who also feel no obligation to be pleasant.

 ALERT!

One way to minimize hurt feelings is to discourage gift-giving at the post-wedding reception—because, after all, it's not a real stretch for these folks to assume that they're only being invited to this event simply because they're expected to bring a present.

If your daughter agrees to the no-gift policy, you're in for smooth sailing. If she's ranting and raving that she needs pots and pans and a colander and money . . . you might just want to call the whole thing off. Her intentions will be transparent to your guests, and as the host, you'll be held at least partly responsible—whether your friends and family choose to express their resentment or simply hold this reception against you for the rest of your life.

Nix the B List

Though it's a risky practice, brides who are having traditional weddings sometimes draw up a list of alternate guests—folks who don't make the cut during the first round of invitations, but who are more than welcome to fill the spaces left vacant by regrets. Why is this risky? Because, often, these guests *realize* that they're on the B List (when they receive their invitations a scant three weeks prior to the wedding) and are greatly offended.

If this is unadvisable where a traditional wedding reception is concerned, it's doubly so for the post-wedding reception. Having a B List for this party effectively means that these folks have been snubbed twice—once when they weren't invited to the actual wedding, and again when they failed to make the first draft of the guest list for this reception. Advise the newlyweds (and anyone else who's tossing names into the ring) to make a list and stick with it.

Invitations for this reception should be sent at least one month before the reception. Must they be formal and engraved? If it's a large, formal reception, you shouldn't send out handwritten invites; you'll need to find a reputable printer in your area. They need not be engraved, though; today's printing techniques are able to mimic the highfalutin look of years gone by at a much more affordable price.

Chapter 8

Topics of Major Consequence

As the Big Day approaches, some of the paternal duties you're incredibly skilled in—like giving advice, lecturing, pointing out the error of your kids' ways—get lost in the shuffle. After all, there's a wedding being planned, and no one has the time to address actual life issues. Still, there might be a thing or two that's bothering you about the whole setup your daughter has going on here . . . must you neglect your duties in the name of being supportive during the wedding season?

How *Could* She?

Your daughter and the man she's planning to marry have decided to move in together before the wedding, and you're just sick over it. This isn't the way you raised her. Nice girls wait until after the wedding to set up house, and that's all there is to it.

 FACT

> Maybe no one is going to change your beliefs on the matter, but this is not something worth threatening to kick her out of the family over. If she's got the ring on her finger, she's obviously pretty serious about spending the rest of her life with this guy—starting *now*.

What you're experiencing is a generation gap. Gone are the days where cohabitation before the wedding day was frowned upon; in fact, these days, it's commonplace for engaged couples to move into a home before the wedding. There are actually a lot of benefits to this setup, starting with the fact that moving in together *after* returning from the honeymoon can be incredibly stressful and hectic. Returning home to an actual home is a piece of cake in comparison. In addition, they'll already know what their monthly living expenses are— they won't be forced to choose between heat and food because they *way* underestimated the gas bill.

That's not to say that you have to like the whole situation. You *do* have to try to understand where your daughter is coming from, though. She's not doing this to hurt you, and she's not trying to bring shame upon the family—she's trying to make her life a little easier, and she's surrounded by hordes of couples who have done the same thing without being struck down by a lightning bolt.

The Second Marriage

Oh, goodness. She's getting ready to walk down that aisle for the second (or third) time, and you're just up in arms over the whole thing. As far as you can tell, she didn't learn anything from her first marriage (which she now refers to as "that one big mistake"). You fear she's jumping into a new life with someone else without even taking stock of what went awry the first time around. What's a dad to do?

 ESSENTIAL

If there's something obviously wrong in her relationship (physical abuse, substance abuse) then you do have an obligation to speak up. Otherwise, you may just have to trust that she knows what she's getting into this time around.

You can't protect her from everything, unfortunately, and if she's made up her mind, chances are she's going to end up as this guy's Mrs. Still, there's no harm in trying to point out some very obvious flaws in her reasoning . . . *if* you know how to do it.

Look at Yourself First

If *you're* divorced, you know the pain and hard feelings that surround the decision—not just from your former spouse, but very possibly from her friends and family as well. Maybe you're so scarred from your own experience that you just can't fathom how—or why—anyone could put themselves in the position to be hurt so badly again (not to mention the *cost* of going through the ordeal).

However, you simply can't judge your daughter's choice to remarry based on your own trauma. She went through a tough time, to be sure, but if she's found someone to share her life with and she's happy, you've got to let your own fears and attitudes concerning marriage fall by the wayside (as far as her relationship is concerned, anyway). People do make mistakes, and sometimes, they even learn from their errors. And *sometimes*, they're able to rise above it all and move on. That's what she's doing.

He's the Same Guy

Huh. So she divorced her first husband because she couldn't stand the guy, and now she's marrying someone who is so similar you suspect they might be long-lost twin brothers. That's a real pickle for you to be in, isn't it? What do you say to a daughter who is entering into the same exact marriage that she couldn't wait to get out of? Do you have to give your blessing? What if you really like him, but you know that she's going to be packing her bags six months after the ceremony?

For starters, you're never obligated to give your blessing to a union that you don't approve of—regardless of how you feel about the groom. Still, if you feel that she's making the same exact mistake she made the first time, yes, you can address the issue with her.

 ALERT!

Be aware that withholding your best wishes may cause real trouble in your relationship with your daughter and carries with it the very real possibility that she'll go ahead and marry him anyway, which will leave you in the dog-house for years to come.

Watch how you phrase your concerns when you bring the matter up for discussion. There's a difference between telling her she's not so bright and she's going to have another failed marriage within a year and simply saying, "Honey, I think we need to talk. Don't you think Ron [the new beau] is an awful lot like Don [the first husband]? Maybe you can tell me what you see in Ron that you didn't see in Don and why this marriage is going to last."

Might she find fault with the latter approach as well? Sure. She's a bride, after all, and probably given to mood swings and overall anxiety. She may even use the time-honored defense, "It's *my* life!" Just remember: You're really, genuinely concerned and trying to help. Even if she flies off the handle and tells you it's none of your business, you'll know that you attempted to get the discussion going. Beyond that, it's up to her.

Hey, It's *Your* Money!

You shelled out some pretty big bucks for the first wedding, and now that she's come home to introduce you to her next husband, she seems to be assuming that you're only too happy to go through the whole check-writing process all over again. Except you aren't.

Hey, you're right—it *is* your money, and if you're not willing (or able at this point) to pay for another big wedding, say so right away. The one thing you'll want to keep to yourself is this opinion (or any variation of it): "I just spent $20,000 on a wedding that was a complete waste! You still haven't finished opening your wedding gifts, and you want me to pay for another wedding?!"

Um . . . no, Dad. That kind of ranting isn't going to win you any fans. Bluntness like that will earn you the Incredibly Insensitive Father label, which will follow you for . . . well, decades. It's the stuff that family legends are born of. If you're feeling a little concerned about how free your daughter seems to be with your money when it comes to weddings, find a better (calmer) way to say it.

FACT

You're not obligated to pay for another grand wedding. If you feel *that* strongly about it, you don't have to give her one single penny to pay for her second wedding—but again, keep in mind, this could affect your relationship with your daughter for a long, long time.

If you're able to give her a little something to put toward her wedding, you may want to mull it over. A flat out refusal to assist financially (when she knows you're using your moneybags as pillows) constitutes a complete disapproval of the union. Maybe your intention is to send that very message; that's your choice, and you already know the risks involved here. If, on the other hand, you simply want her to realize the value of a buck by forcing her to pay for a wedding that *she* can afford, that's a whole other conversation.

Your Image

She's getting married again, and you're red-faced. What is she doing with her life, you wonder? Her first husband seemed like a good guy to you, but she claimed she was unhappy. Now she's been looking around, trying to find a situation that's perfect for her, and she claims this new guy is The One. For sure.

You, quite frankly, are a little embarrassed. How did you raise such a flighty kid? What will everyone think when they get the invitation to your capricious daughter's second wedding?

You know what? You need to forget about everyone else. You can't live your life worrying about what other people will think, because you can't ever make everyone happy, or impress everyone at the same time.

 ESSENTIAL

As a dad, you're supposed to impart this wisdom to your own kids—and judging from your daughter's attempts to make her life better regardless of the opinions of the masses, you might just have succeeded in this matter.

If your daughter has just gotten divorced and she's sprinting to the altar with a guy she met in her divorce lawyer's office, you're right to be concerned. These issues are best dealt with by asking a professional for help—it could be that your daughter has self-esteem issues or that she simply isn't mature enough to realize the gravity of taking on a new marriage. If, on the other hand, she left her first marriage some time ago and she's not rushing into this new marriage, you're just going to have to give her credit for knowing what she wants. She is an adult, after all.

They've Got Kids

Of course, the issue of marriage and remarriage and how it affects your daughter is one of the smaller concerns when there are kids involved. Though stepfamilies are hardly unusual these days, making the move from planning the future to actually being involved in a whole new family dynamic isn't easy on most blended clans. You're in a tough spot, Grandpa (or Step-Grandpa). You're watching from the sidelines, hoping that everything turns out all right.

Her Kids

Your grandchildren are getting a new stepfather, and possibly some stepsiblings—along with the whole kit and kaboodle of step relatives. If the kids seem to be making the adjustment well, count your blessings. However, if you sense there's trouble afoot (the kids are reluctant to even talk about the wedding, for example, or are all too eager to bash the groom and his brood), you're probably losing some sleep over the matter. At the very least, you are wondering what—if any—responsibilities you have in this matter. Should a grandparent butt in during this situation?

Every set of circumstances will be different, of course,

but in the end, there's really not a whole lot you can do. You can't stop the wedding; you can't take your grandkids away from your daughter; and if you overstep your boundaries (by telling your daughter that her choices are hurting her kids), you may never see those kids again. The best thing that you can do is to let your grandchildren know that you support them and that you're there if they need you. Be *their* rock.

They'll probably need you a lot in the months following the wedding, if everyone in their home is really having a tough time getting used to each other. Try not to blatantly take sides on any one issue, but also avoid playing devil's advocate too much—especially with teenagers. What these kids need is to know that someone really cares what they're going through; they need a sounding board.

His Kids

Of course, the wedding could make you an instant grandparent if your childless daughter is marrying a man with kids from another relationship. How do you handle *that* one?

It's fairly easy to look at these kids as having nothing to do with you—after all, they aren't your grandkids, and you don't expect to have a whole lot to do with them after the wedding, especially if they've already got a set (or two) of biological grandparents. You could be right on the money here, and that may be exactly the way things work out for you in this situation—but it doesn't have to be that way. Here's where having an open mind will really help matters.

Children aren't limited to accepting the love and guidance of blood relatives. The definition of "family" has been revised (several times, in fact) over the past few decades, and now, this marriage between your daughter and her groom makes you part of their melded group of relatives.

 ESSENTIAL

> Don't rule out the idea of treating these kids as part of the family. The benefits to everyone are obvious—you'll probably see more of your daughter, and the kids will have another responsible adult in their lives.

All right, you're thinking, so what if your new son-in-law's kids don't want to have one thing to do with you? Depending on their ages, you might be fighting a losing battle. Teenagers are notoriously difficult creatures, sometimes never more so than in situations of remarriage. You obviously can't force kids to accept you as part of the family, and if they're truly awful, leave them alone. Give them their space, and fight the urge to return any rudeness in kind. Given time, they may come around—or they may not, but it's vital for them to see you acting like an adult.

Their Kids

So the kids have been around for a while, and their parents are just now deciding to tie the knot. Everyone's happy, right?

Hey, why aren't you smiling, Dad? Is it that you're worried that this marriage just isn't right—that your daughter and her beau are getting married for the sake of the kids, and not because they're in love?

Maybe you just *know* that this marriage is doomed—there's constant backbiting going on, and they just seem to be completely unprepared for a lifelong commitment to each other. You're probably right to be concerned. Above all else, you don't want to see your grandkids put into a situation that's going to end badly.

 FACT

Keep in mind that you're not in the relationship. You can't really know what goes on between your daughter and her groom-to-be. They may have a different way of showing their affection, or they may be very reserved in public. Everything behind the scenes could be just fine.

Here's the bad news: There's nothing you can do about it. Depending on your relationship with your daughter, you may be able to broach the subject and ask her what she hopes to gain in this marriage. If she comes right out and tells you she's only doing it for the kids, that's obviously a red flag and warrants further discussion. But if she's bound and determined to go through with this marriage, you obviously can't stop her. You'll be there to help hold your grandkids together if things don't go according to the best-laid plans. That's your job as Grandpa, and you'll do it well if you're called upon.

You've Got Company

Why, look who's at the door. It's your daughter, and she wants to know if she and her fiancé can maybe just set up house with you after the wedding. (Seems as though you *won't* be converting her bedroom into an office after all.) They want to be with you, she says, because you're the coolest dad ever. Plus your house is a lot nicer than any of the apartments they've seen so far.

So you weren't planning on having the newlyweds living in your home. Are you the meanest dad alive if you put your foot down and say, "No, no, no, absolutely not"? Or are you simply guarding your own privacy and mental health? (Even the most progressive dads realize that newlyweds are in love and need to snuggle up with each other all the time, regardless of who's present in the room.)

Don't Unpack!

Hopefully, your daughter and her new husband won't show up at your house with their bags and their wedding gifts in tow. Ideally, there would be a conversation prior to the newlyweds setting up camp in your home, during which you'll be given the opportunity to accept the idea or to gently crush their hopes of saving money on rent.

 ALERT!

If you plan on saying no to their request to move in, telling them sooner rather than later is best. You won't have to deal with the guilt of having one of them say, "Well, we just gave up a great, cheap apartment because we thought you would let us move in!"

You might want to point out to them that living on their own has many benefits:

- Privacy—which every newlywed couple needs.
- Independence. Living in one's own home fosters a sense of (almost) complete freedom.
- Responsibility. Being forced to pay one's own bills encourages mature financial decision making.

Though the promise of reaping these benefits may be hard for the couple to swallow right now, you shouldn't feel guilty about not wanting to share your home. After all, by getting married, they were implying that they're ready to take on their fair share of adult responsibilities—starting with setting up their own household. Just don't string them along, letting them think that you're going to agree to this deal, when you know there's just no way you're ever going to think this is a suitable arrangement.

Plenty of Room!

Of course, you may actually love the idea of having the kids under your roof—and in many families, it's the norm to have everyone living together. The benefit of this? It certainly creates a sense of one for all, and all for one. To make the arrangement a successful one, however, everyone has to pitch in and do his or her share.

If you're a first-timer at this, some issues you may want to address include:

Rent. Will you expect the kids to pay for their room and board? What about utilities? Or will you go to some other kind of arrangement? (They'll do the cooking and the cleaning, and you'll pay for the groceries.)

Privacy issues. Are there certain areas of your home that are off-limits (such as your bedroom or home office)? The newlyweds will probably expect that you'll stay out of their quarters, as well.

Visitors. Will the kids be allowed to host friends in your home, or do you value your peace and quiet?

Communication issues. Make a plan for resolving problems before they arise. You could set up a weekly powwow during which concerns can be addressed, or you could simply agree to have open and honest negotiations as needed.

Communication is the most important issue to address. Cohabitation works very well for some families, but not if everyone is sitting around mumbling under their breath about what so-and-so is doing (or not doing). If you can all talk openly about any sticking points, you might just make a go of having the whole family under one roof. And if things go badly . . . the door is always there.

They're Broke

Of course, the issue of whether or not to let the kids move into your home takes on an entirely different slant when they come to you and tell you that unless you let them in, they're going to be sleeping on the streets.

 ESSENTIAL

Feeling guilted into letting the newlyweds live with you because they can't afford to live on their own? It's all right to be forthcoming with your expectations of them, including an estimated date of their permanent departure.

Oh . . . you saw this coming months ago, before the wedding, and you didn't say anything about it at the time. You figured that since they were getting married, they had to have some sort of plan for paying their bills. It must have slipped their minds in between all of the wedding planning and asking you for blank checks to cover the cost of the caterer and florist. How could this have ended differently? If you could go back and do anything to help them avoid this point, what would it be?

Poke Your Nose In . . . A Little

Well, for starters, if your daughter has only recently announced her engagement, it's not too late for you to get in on this game. No, she doesn't have to tell you how much money she and her groom have set aside for after the wedding, but you might want some kind of assurance there is some fund, somewhere, to ensure their entry into the World of Independent Living after they're married—especially if neither of them has left the safety of their parents' homes prior to the ceremony.

Lay it out for them: monthly expenses versus their earnings. Be as harsh and as realistic as you need to be in order to get your point across. You're not hurting them by being honest—you're actually helping them to get a handle on the realities of married life before they hit some pretty hard times. You'd hate to see them go out and buy a luxury sports coupe only to have them realize—too late—that they *should* have spent their wedding money on the two month's deposit for a new apartment.

Oh, All Right . . . Come In

If it becomes clear to you that there's just no way these two are going to make it on their own—at least not in the foreseeable future—allowing them to take up residence in your home instead of having them fight for space at the homeless shelter is a generous move on your part. They should be very grateful, and it's all right for you to point that out (once) if they've moved in and started acting as though they're the new co-owners.

Ideally, there should be a time limit as to how long you're willing to let them stay. This will take the pressure off of you six months down the road, when things are looking much better for them financially and you're starting to wonder when the heck they'll want to move out (*never* is the answer, unless you light that fire underneath them). This also forces them to take stock of their areas of greatest concern, whether it be finding a job or finding a reasonably priced flat outside the city limits.

 FACT

While you're shooting for common understanding and respect between parties, you don't have to take a lot of guff from the people you're helping. Likewise, you shouldn't make them feel bad about their inability to pay their own bills.

Verbal Grenades

A dad who allows a couple of newlyweds to move into his home because they're flat broke is different from the dad who *wants* the kids under his roof. This may be a very hard decision for you to make, because you want them to learn their own life lessons, and yet you can't have your little girl sleeping on a park bench. You may blame her new husband, you may question whether they have any business being married, and you may be hostile toward one or both of them for putting you in a spot you'd rather not be in. You may feel like venting all these frustrations. However, that's probably not a good idea if you expect to live under one roof with them for a while.

While communication is the key to living in peace, there's a difference between communicating and nitpicking. The former involves matters of fact: how much they're expected to pay in rent or utilities; whether they are expected to run some errands, if you're allowing one of them to use your car. The latter involves a whole lot of complaining about issues that aren't all that important in the big picture: they paid you in fives and tens and they know you prefer twenties; your daughter bought the generic toilet paper at the store instead of the name-brand; your son-in-law used the car and didn't tune the radio back to your favorite station.

Herewith, a list of topics that are off limits to you if you're fuming over having to share your home with kids who should have known better than to attempt life on their own:

Their jobs. Assuming they have jobs, it's not up to you to critique the quality of their positions. If they're working hard and meeting their end of any financial agreement you've made with them, back off.

Their marriage. Again, not for you to judge. Maybe they *didn't* have any idea what they were getting into—but they're learning right now, for sure. Your telling them how young and naïve they are isn't going to help matters.

Their personal habits. All right, if your son-in-law insists on cutting his toenails in the living room, that's fair game. The way he eats his pizza (by picking off the cheese so that he might eat it separately from the crust) is not. Eat at different times if it's really getting to you.

The future of your relationship with your daughter and your son-in-law could well hinge on how well all of you are able to settle disputes. You can only control *your* behavior, of course. But if you're respectful of them, you have every right to expect them to return the favor—and to expect things to proceed as smoothly as possible.

Chapter 9

Tribal Relations

Fathers of the bride, even the best and luckiest of the bunch, do not exist in a vacuum. By your very title, you're included in some sort of family structure—for better or for worse. Here's where life catches up with you, even if you've been fairly successful in avoiding certain family members (or *former* family members) for years. A wedding brings everyone together— relatives who love each other and those who despise one another—and expects everyone to let bygones be bygones.

Your Ex

You kissed your wife goodbye many, many moons ago, and you never regretted the decision. You've both been much happier in the years since, and in fact, if you didn't have a daughter in common, you would never think about the woman at all. Now that your child is getting married, you've been forced to consider your former wife, and her new husband, and your former in-laws . . . and whether all of you can come together peacefully.

Be a Big Person

No matter what went on between you and your ex, you have to leave it in the past for now. If there are still legal issues dragging on and on (and on), it's going to be very difficult, to say the least, and this will probably be the ultimate test of your emotional strength. If you're having a hard time being anywhere near the woman, be frank with your daughter—but be careful not to put her in a tough spot. She's already been through the wringer of your divorce, and she's on precarious emotional ground as a bride, anyway.

Asking your daughter not to schedule wedding-planning meetings that necessitate the presence of both you and her mother is well within your limits. Requesting that the two of you not be seated at the same table during the reception is all right, too—as long as you don't follow up your request with a thirty-minute diatribe against old Mom.

Now, if your divorce was amicable and the two of you are old chums at this point, your daughter will proceed with the planning as she sees fit. If you're somewhere in the middle, your daughter will greatly appreciate your making the effort to be pleasant to one another.

 ALERT!

> Don't even think about badmouthing the bride's mother, as this will only make you look petty and inconsiderate. This is about your daughter and her wedding; your issues with her mom aren't something that she should hear about in great detail at any time, and especially not now.

You're Out; Mom's In

Regardless of how close you are to your daughter, you may find yourself on the outside of the wedding-planning extravaganza if you've been divorced from her mother. It's just natural for a girl to want (and need) her mom around her at this time, and you might have a very hard time jockeying for space alongside the bride.

You're hurt, and you have every right to be—don't you? Well . . . yes and no. Your daughter isn't intentionally trying to make you feel bad, and that should count for something.

It's likely that she's depending on her mother more than you at this point because—political correctness aside—mothers and daughters are more apt to get excited about making themselves pretty and planning a lavish party, while dads are often *less* interested.

 FACT

> Your daughter needs someone who's genuinely interested in dress shopping and discussing the merits of strapless bras and slingback high heels to help her right now; chances are, her mother fits that bill better than you do.

So try not to think of it in terms of whom your daughter loves best, because *she* isn't thinking that way. This is just one of those situations where it's easy for you to be left behind because of your gender and because of the surrounding circumstances. Your daughter has great plans for you down the road (on her actual wedding day).

New Guy in Town

So your ex-wife has herself a new husband—or one that's been around for years. Regardless of his tenure, he's there, and now that this wedding has popped up, you have to deal with the guy—somehow. Whether you actually acknowledge his presence or not, you're making a statement about your state of mind and how big of a person you're willing to be.

Understandably, there are circumstances that can't be forgiven or forgotten. If this new guy kind of nudged his way into the family before there was any talk of divorce between you and your ex, your feelings may be very different from the man whose ex-wife remarried ten years after the split. That's between you and him, and this book would never presume to counsel you on mending that rift.

What this book will advise you to do, though, is to find a way to coexist with your daughter's stepfather, even if the sight of him makes your blood boil. Remember: This is a joyous occasion for your little girl, regardless of *your* personal life. You're keeping the peace for her, and she'll appreciate it (and she definitely will hold it *against* you if you spend her wedding day staring down your ex's new man—so don't).

 ESSENTIAL

Try not to feel snubbed by your daughter's decision to include her stepfather—he's obviously played an important role in her life, and it's not up to you to question the validity of her feelings.

And then again, there are plenty of former and current husbands who get along pretty well—or at least well enough to occupy the same space in a banquet hall for a few hours. You may be sharing the father of the bride duties with him, depending on how long he's been in your daughter's life and/or how close she is to him. This is your daughter's decision in the end, so try to go with the flow here. Dividing duties with the bride's stepdad doesn't mean that you can't be every bit as charming and debonair as you would have been if you were the *only* father of the bride in attendance at the wedding. You may be sharing the spotlight with him, but there's room enough there for both of you to be irresistibly witty and downright enchanting—to one another and to all of the guests.

Your Former Family

Alas, a divorce also affects your relationship with your former in-laws. If you've been labeled as That Bad Man by your ex-wife's family since the breakup, you may be feeling nervous about seeing them—or you may be feeling as though you're willing to take on anyone who dares to treat you badly at your daughter's wedding, as it's neither the time nor the place to beat dead horses. Who do they think they are, anyway?

You have a point. A wedding is a horrible place to carry on old grudge matches—but it takes two to wrestle. Refusing to hit below the belt may well eliminate you from the game altogether. Then again, you may have more abuse heaped upon you because you're good enough not to engage in such behavior at your daughter's wedding.

So what if you're taking a lot of verbal abuse in the form of snide comments and dirty looks from your ex's side of the family? As the host of this wedding, you have every right to expect a little respect from your guests. As adults, they should know better than to sully this joyous occasion with old issues.

 QUESTION

> **Am I within my rights to tell an offensive guest to shape up or ship out?**
> Only if the offense is substantial enough. You should be able to ignore your ex-mother-in-law's dirty stares; if she throws a drink in your face, however, she's ruining your daughter's party, and should be shown the door.

Your New Wife versus Your Daughter

Now, if *you're* the one who has remarried, you could find yourself in the midst of tense interventions, running back and forth between interested parties and trying to keep the peace in your own home when your new wife feels she's been snubbed. How are you supposed to handle this? (After all, you're one man—and though you are reluctant to admit it, you *don't* have superpowers.)

Why Can't They Just Get Along?

There's not a harder situation in the world to be in than the one that puts you in the middle of your new wife and your little princess. You love 'em both, so why can't they just learn to love each other? (Heck, you'd settle for them *tolerating* one another on the first Tuesday of every other month.)

The fact of the matter is, you and your ex-wife have your own issues that have either been worked out by this point or have been left to fester. Your daughter has been affected by your divorce in one way or another, whether she admits it or not, and depending on the circumstances involved, may have chosen a side by this point. If she chose your ex-wife's side, she's probably acting out against *you* by snubbing your new wife.

 FACT

There are some women who simply don't like each other. It could be that your daughter and your wife are on opposing sides of every issue, regardless of its importance in the greater scheme of life.

Then there are always the kids who, even as adults, see no reason why their divorced parents shouldn't get back together, and view any new spouse as an intruder who's just mucking things up. So many issues! So little you can do about them!

Your Role Here

You can't force your daughter and your wife to like each other. What you do have a right to insist on, in this case, and especially if you're paying for the wedding, is that your daughter *respect* your wife, and vice versa. They don't have to become best friends, but they should be able to put their feelings aside—for now, anyway—because by carrying a load of hatred around, they're hurting *themselves* more than they're hurting each other.

Stepsibling Rivalry

Unfortunately, your Stepkids + Your Biological Children = Disaster. The situation, while perhaps under control at this point, is not what you'd call amicable. It's more along the lines of "you stay in your corner of the world and I'll stay in mine," which itself took plenty of time for the kids (who are now technically adults) to work out. In other words, as long as they don't have to interact with each other, everything's groovy between them.

Should They Be Invited?

Your daughter has now raised the valid point that she's having a smallish wedding and she doesn't want to exclude people she actually likes from the guest list just so her stepsiblings can be invited. Plus, she's sure the stepsiblings won't come anyway, so no harm done. You want to say something about this, but *what*?

For starters, if you're paying for the wedding and you want your stepkids included, they're in. That's one of the perks of being the host. Of course, if you're only paying for part of the gala (or your daughter and her beau are footing the entire bill themselves), negotiations will be necessary. Even though everything your daughter is saying may be right on the mark (you're fairly certain that the stepsiblings won't show up, and there is a very limited amount of space available in the reception facility), you should still try to convince her that inviting her stepbrother(s) and/or stepsister(s) is the right thing to do.

 ALERT!

> No matter what the relationship between the two camps, excluding members of the family from the wedding guest list is pretty harsh, and something that will be held against your daughter—and probably you, as well—for the rest of eternity.

Long-Term Effects

Excluding family members from weddings is the kind of thing that becomes family folklore. The story the stepsiblings will tell each other—and their friends and their other family members—goes something like this: "Janie is coldhearted. I always knew it, but not inviting us to her wedding just proved it beyond the shadow of a doubt." This will be followed by other anecdotes exemplifying Janie's negative attributes and will be summed up by a group decision to never forgive her. Ever.

Offering the stepsibs the chance to attend (or to refuse to attend) the wedding takes the pressure off of you, at least. They may decide not to come, after all, in which case you and your daughter can both honestly say that you made the effort to include them.

Your Estranged, Engaged Daughter

You got the call: Your little girl is getting married. You obviously wish her the best, but since you haven't been involved in her life for years, you're wondering what she wants or expects from you at this point, as far as the wedding is concerned. You feel sort of bad about reentering her life simply because she's getting married (because, in fact, you've been meaning to get in touch with her for . . . well, a long time), but since she's the one who initiated the contact, she must want you around for this.

Getting Back in Touch

If she is the one who came looking for you, then your assumption is correct. She wouldn't have tracked you down to let you know about her marriage if she didn't want to reconnect with you. Consider yourself a lucky man and seize the opportunity. If you've been less than responsible in your relationship with your daughter up 'til this point, resolve to change your ways. A lot of distant dads don't get a second chance to make things right.

That being said, you may have no idea what's important to a bride/daughter and what isn't. Start with this list:

Timely communications. If she calls you on Monday and asks you to call her back, don't wait two weeks. Return the call ASAP.

Honesty. Don't tell her that you have all sorts of contacts and can get her a great deal on all of her wedding expenses unless (and until) you're 100 percent positive that you can. Nothing turns an adult kid off faster than a dad who's all talk.

Openness. Especially if you've been out of contact for some time, get to know her again. And let go of your preconceived notions of who she is. (She may have been into gymnastics the last time you saw her, but now she might be into investment banking.)

Respect for her boundaries. Even though *she* came knocking on *your* door, she may still have some serious issues with your relationship. Don't expect too much too soon.

Don't Jump in Too Quickly

Be sure you weigh the situation carefully. If your daughter hasn't actually come looking for you, but you've heard through the grapevine she's engaged, you may feel the urge to give her a call and get back into her life. Your instincts are half-right.

Giving her a call or sending her a card wishing her well is great. After all, *not* acknowledging her engagement is the only other option, and it's not a smart one, even if it's been your pattern all these years to ignore big family news. But making the assumption that she wants you enmeshed in her life at this point (because, after all, she's going to need you to walk her down the aisle—or so you think) may be completely wrong.

 FACT

> Extending your good wishes to her is enough, for now. She'll know where you are, and she'll know you're well aware of her impending nuptials. If she responds positively to your overtures, you're doing well. If she doesn't, you can't force it.

Keeping the Peace

Too many times, family members make the mistake of presuming that a wedding will heal old wounds and clear the path for a happy future together. That's a lot to expect from one event; family ties need time to strengthen themselves. That's not to say that your daughter's engagement can't be the impetus for family healing—just don't set your sights unrealistically high. Take it slow, and you'll have a better shot at establishing a new, better relationship with her.

How can you convince your family to stop the fighting and ensure a smooth wedding season for everyone when the planning requires all of you to be in the same room?

Lay the ground rules down to everyone who's involved:

- Raised voices will not be tolerated.
- No name calling.
- You will act fairly as moderator (even if the thought of doing so scares the living daylights out of you).
- Each person will be able to finish his or her thought before someone else speaks.

If all else fails . . . stay away from each other. There's nothing wrong with keeping separate camps during this time. It will require a big effort on your part, but sometimes it's the only way to get things done.

The Groom's Family

They're lovable, they're wacky, and they're your daughter's new in-laws! Or maybe you don't find them so lovable . . . but the wacky part is right on. You're trying to plan a wedding with these people, and things are either going well or not so well. What's your role and your responsibility as far as getting friendly with these folks goes?

Don't Push It

Just because your respective children have somehow managed to find each other in this world doesn't mean that you and the groom's family are going to be instant best friends, or even instant allies. You can't force a friendship, obviously, even if you feel it's in everyone's best interests.

If you're the outgoing, gregarious type and you sense that the groom's parents are much more reserved, you may actually intimidate them with your chatter, even though your intention is simply to encourage good will toward one another. If the situation is reversed—you're the one who is constantly subjected to a nonstop litany of their lives—you may feel as though spending an evening with these people is akin to experiencing hell firsthand.

 ESSENTIAL

> Obviously, you can't force someone to change his or her behavior; you can, of course, change yours, or at least try to modify your own reaction to conduct you initially dislike.

Just remember, your contact with the groom's parents is probably going to be relatively short-lived. You'll be forced to have contact with them while the wedding is being planned. Afterwards, that contact will dwindle down to occasional sightings at your daughter's home, at which time, you'll realize that they're not half as bad as you previously thought they were—or at least they aren't so bad in thirty-minute increments.

For now, give them a wide margin to err within—let some things roll off your back even if you would normally take issue with them. No one will benefit from a hostile relationship between the two sets of parents. Do your part—in fact, do more than your part—to see that things remain on an even keel between you and your daughter's future in-laws.

Work It Out

As different as you may be from one another, during the whole planning of the wedding, you're going to have to find a way to work out those differences in a way that doesn't send your daughter to bed with a migraine. Or in tears. What does this mean to you?

It means that there can't be any shouting matches between you and the groom's parents, and there can't be any badmouthing going on, either. You're all adults, remember, and you're supposed to set a good example for the kids.

 ALERT!

You don't want your daughter to look back on this time in her life—a time that's supposed to be *happy, happy, happy*, by the way—and remember how she had to play referee between the two sets of parents.

"Easier said than done," you're thinking. "You don't know these people I'm dealing with." And you may be right—but do it anyway.

Even if you find yourself in a worst-case situation where the groom's parents are bitter, disagreeable, patronizing folk, don't engage in combat with them directly. If they've treated you *very* badly, then you have every right to keep yourself out of their crosshairs, and you *are* allowed to speak to your daughter about this, but only if you promise yourself beforehand to limit your grievances. (You can't go on and on about how the groom's mother condescendingly called you a *common laborer* and then point out that you hate the woman's hair, too. One point is important; the other isn't. Your daughter should be told about the former complaint; chances are, the two of you are in tacit agreement on the latter point.)

Don't Assume the Worst

If you're from very different places in life (you're a mogul, and the groom's dad is a mechanic—or vice versa), your first inclination may be to assume that there's just no way you can be friendly with this other guy. You have nothing in common, and that's just the way it is.

Depending on which situation you're in, that attitude can be perceived as arrogant or as a sure sign of insecurity. The fact is everyone is human, right? It's everyone's right to be treated with respect, and *not* because of his occupation. Don't assume that the groom's dad is unintelligent because he's blue-collar;

that's incredibly arrogant. Likewise, don't assume he's unapproachable because he's worth a whole lot of dough—that's insecure.

 ESSENTIAL

Give the groom's dad a fair chance before you make any judgments of his character; you might just find that the two of you have more in common than you thought—but you'll never know if you don't give him a fair shake.

Your Other Daughters

Sisters are a funny lot. They love each other, and at the same time, they envy each other. Many sisters fall into a pattern of keeping score—with each other (for past transgressions and remuneration) and with other family members (namely you and your wife and what you've given each of them). You think that's ridiculous? Ask them what each of them got for Christmas in 1985 (assuming they were all present and accounted for at the time). While they may not list every single item, one of them will inevitably peep up and say, "Oh, that's the year *she* got the dollhouse she wanted and *I* got books."

Oh, Great. *Now* You're Rich

Sometimes, your good fortune is a thorn in the side of the eldest child who feels as though she's being cheated out of a whole lot because you used to be broke, but when her sisters came along, you suddenly had money to buy them anything they wanted. You *thought* your financial success was good for the whole family, but apparently, you didn't take this little matter under advisement.

If one daughter has already had a modest wedding—because it was what you could afford at the time—and another daughter is planning to be married soon (now that you're referred to, in certain circulations, as a *tycoon*), you may be in for some resentment from the already married daughter.

Ideally, she will look at the situation rationally and say to herself, "Dad's always been as good to me as he could be. It's nobody's fault that he wasn't incredibly rich when I got married. He gave me what he could." It's *possible*, though, that the voices she's hearing will be saying something more like, "He always liked Sally better. Of course she's going to have everything she wants for her wedding, when I had to cut corners everywhere."

Before you go dismissing her claims of your playing favorites as unreasonable, try to see it from her point of view for just a minute. Is it possible that, monetary issues aside, you *have* favored her sister a bit? Have you always expected more from your older daughter, for example, while the younger one was given much more leeway? It's a common thing that parents do—they tend to see their younger children as babies and older children as little adults.

How does that explanation help you? What's done is done, and you can't go back and change history. Nor would it be fair to cheat your engaged daughter out of her dream wedding just because her married sister is peeved. What you *can* do is to be more sensitive to the issue in the future. Try to see your daughters as adults— no matter what their age or birth order—and treat them as such. Hold them to the same standards; don't baby one and play tough guy with the other. Even as adults, kids sense favoritism—and it hurts them just as badly in their twenties and thirties as it did in elementary school.

 ALERT!

If money is a touchy subject for your daughter (who is still longing for the doll she never got because it was too expensive, even though her little sister got everything *she* ever wanted), the potential for an emotional explosion triples when the treasure in question is actually a wedding.

Unlucky in Love

But what if this is the first wedding in the family, and another daughter is just plain jealous of her sister's impending marriage? Or, worse, what if one sister has been through a divorce and is miserable at the prospect of seeing her sister so content with her life? A lot of dads would pretend this wasn't even happening, because then they wouldn't have to deal with it. And a lot of dads would just deal with it badly, because they would be insensitive to the jealous daughter. Fortunately, *your* girls got the pick of the daddy litter.

 FACT

> There are some daughter-versus-daughter situations that are relatively easy to deal with, such as a younger daughter who is suddenly acting bratty because she's gotten lost in the shuffle of the family's involvement in the older daughter's wedding. (The right answer: Give her some attention.)

Can you really help a daughter who is struggling to accept her bad luck (whether it's real or a figment of her imagination) while being forced to watch her sister's perfect life? That depends on the daughter, and also on her situation.

A more difficult situation would find you trying to balance the emotions of your engaged daughter and her unlucky-in-love sister, who has supposedly sworn off men and who also hasn't accepted the fact that others around her aren't mourning her lost relationship. In this instance, she might really need (and, for all you know, appreciate) a heart-to-heart talk from you. She's an adult, but right now, she may need her dad to tell her that everything really is going to be all right eventually, and that no matter how badly she feels right now, it's no excuse to act badly around her sister. She isn't to blame, after all.

Will you feel as though you're settling arguments the way you did when they were *truly* kids? Sure. But that's your job, and you're good at it.

Chapter 10
Creative Gift Giving

You've done your bit by getting involved in the planning and by presenting two broad shoulders for your daughter to cry on occasionally. You've tried on the tux; you've even agreed to wear it. You've worked on the guest list, you've gotten in touch with long lost relatives, and through it all, you've kept your sense of humor. Are you finished yet? Almost. Now you'll need to give some thought as to what kind of gift—if any—you're going to present to the newlyweds.

The Thought Process

Fathers of the bride often fall into two camps—those who are overly generous, and those who aren't. Now, before your feelings are bruised by that statement, realize that zealous generosity is as much a state of mind as it is a financial situation. In other words, if you would love to give your daughter the world but you just can't afford the price tag on it, it really is the thought that counts.

Following this logic, some fathers will want to top off their daughter's wedding by giving her and her new hubby a gift that will evoke a strong reaction from the couple—whether it's an excited whoop of joy or tears of sentimentality. Other fathers will consider their time and monetary contribution toward the wedding gift enough—and perhaps rightly so, if these men have really gone out on a limb, financially and otherwise, to help pull the wedding together.

 FACT

It's all right to feel as though you have nothing left to give—because, after all, weddings are incredibly expensive. However, if it's anywhere within your reach, you may want to commemorate the occasion with some sort of wedding gift for the newlyweds.

What Kind of Gift?

So what passes as an appropriate wedding gift from father to daughter these days? Well, just like everything else in the modern wedding arena, anything goes. If you've got a great gift idea swirling around in your head, go with it; heartfelt gifts are always the best ones. However, if you're at a complete loss, remember—you can really give them *anything*. To narrow down the choices, ask yourself these questions:

- What do the newlyweds need?
- What do they want?
- What can't they afford at this point?

Of course, the answers to each of these questions may be different. They may need a set of salt and pepper shakers; they may want a big screen TV, and they may not be able to afford much of anything at this point. You need to prioritize what type of gift you'd like to hand over and then follow that trail.

If you have no idea what they want or need, check their registry. It should be updated with every purchase that's been made, and you'll be able to quickly see which items have been scooped up by other well-wishers and which are still on the wish list.

Something for the Home

Let's say the newlyweds have already moved into a home, and they have everything they need, really, except . . . there's *something* missing. Do the blank walls disturb you, or is it the way that *nothing* matches? Can their neighbors see right in the windows for the simple reason that there isn't a curtain to be had in the house? Here's where you can provide them with something they really need and give a gift they'll appreciate.

Consider giving them a good piece of artwork to hang in their entryway, or over the sofa—anyplace that needs a little sprucing up. Take a good look at their color scheme (if they have one, that is) and choose something appropriate. Newlyweds generally love romantic pictures or sculptures of couples holding one another, or staring into one another's eyes, but you can go against that grain if you'd rather purchase a serene painting of an English garden or a depiction of small-town America.

 ALERT!

Make sure that the artwork you're giving fits the newlyweds' overall taste. Your contemporary-minded daughter may simply roll her eyes at an ultraconservative choice and hang it only when you're coming for a visit.

Hire a Designer

Not into giving art? How about hiring an interior designer for a consultation with the newlyweds? This is a rather pricey service that many young homeowners would love to have, but would never consider paying for. Some designers charge by the hour; others charge by the room or project.

 FACT

> If you were to hire your designer to do some of his fancy home-work, you would purchase furniture, curtains, or other materials through him, and your final bill would include his commission on these items.

One caveat about interior designers or decorators: Find someone who is used to dealing with the type of project you're looking at (e.g., a starter home). A higher-priced expert may have incredible ideas, but it's just as likely that he or she normally only works in multimillion dollar homes. Even if you somehow managed to lasso him into your daughter's bungalow, his thoughts of tearing out walls and commissioning giant paintings may be completely unrealistic, both for the home itself and for the budget you're working with. If the chemistry is all wrong between the two of you (or is completely, suspiciously absent), keep looking.

Where will you find the man or the woman with the plans? Word of mouth is always a safe bet. If you have friends who have recently worked with a designer, ask them about their experience. You might also want to visit home shows or model homes in the area where decorators show off their talents. Your local chamber of commerce might also be able to flip you a reputable designer or two.

You'll want to ask designers about their training and you want to contact some former clients for references. Make sure their contractors (painters, for example) are insured. Above all, don't be afraid to lay everything on the line—the size of the project, the budget, and the deadline (if any). You're spending good money on their services; make sure you're getting what you want.

 ESSENTIAL

Most newlyweds would love to have a cleaning or cooking service. Treat your daughter to a month's vacation from these chores. You're giving the new couple the gift of time—time to relax and unwind and settle into married life.

More Human Help

A professional organizer is another expert who is considered a rather luxurious (though very necessary, in some homes) expense. This person comes in, literally cleans house, throws out what the couple doesn't need, and organizes the things that they absolutely must have (such as dishes and clothes). Not an inexpensive gift, but something that the newlyweds would probably love.

If the newlyweds are living in a new home without even the promise of shrubbery, think about hiring a landscaping service for them. While this is also a fairly expensive venture, you may be able to at least get them *started* with some greenery, and a little landscaping can make a huge difference in a home's appearance (especially if the alternative is a bare yard).

Hobbies and Interests

Are the newlyweds into outdoor activities? Are they buying a new home? Do they like to travel? Do they have to be seated in a theater every Saturday night? Couples who are involved in distinct activities are incredibly easy to buy for. Take a good look at what they love to do . . . and then gift wrap something.

For the outdoor enthusiasts, consider a canoe, sleeping bags, a good tent, a kayak, snowshoes . . . whatever floats their boat. New homeowners need everything: lawn equipment, ladders, tools. Travelers will appreciate good luggage or a trip to just about anywhere. Season tickets to a good theater will excite show lovers.

Of course, you aren't limited to the activities that the couple is already immersed in; after all, if they're avid theatergoers, they may have very distinct preferences; if they've traveled around the world already, they probably don't need much in the way of baggage. In this case, you have to start thinking a little differently.

Have they always wanted to try something new, something different? Maybe they could both use a few cooking lessons; maybe scuba lessons would thrill them. Perhaps they'd really love a hot-air balloon ride or the chance to skydive on your dime. Open up a new horizon for them; they'll always remember it was you who got them started. (And if they don't follow through with years of enjoyment of this activity, it will at the very least have been an unforgettable gift.)

 FACT

> While it is the thought that counts, remember that this is a wedding gift. Get as personal as you can with it.

Traditional Wedding Gifts

Nothing's grabbing you, huh? You're a tough customer, Mister. If these gift ideas just aren't *you*, then you're probably in a more traditional mindset—which is just fine. Any bride who has gone to the trouble to plan a traditional wedding will be thrilled with a traditional gift (and probably has a few in mind).

Personalize It

Most newlyweds love anything monogrammed or engraved. A set of bar glasses (the *whole* set—not just the highballs or the beer mugs) with their joint initials is something they'll appreciate for years to come. Monogrammed linens are another nice choice. An engraved picture frame with their initials or their newly married title ("The Browns") will come in handy—they'll be displaying their wedding photos as soon as they have them in their hands.

There are many, many monogramming options. You might choose to use a single initial (your daughter's first name or her husband's surname), you could use your daughter's maiden name, or you might choose to intertwine the newlyweds' names. For example, Ellen White, who has married Andrew Brown, might receive linens monogrammed in any of the following ways: *EBA* (wife's first, husband's last, husband's first initials); *ABE* (husband's first and last followed by wife's first initial); or *W.B* (surnames separated by a period or some sort of embroidery).

 FACT

If your daughter is keeping her maiden name and you'd like to include both the bride's and groom's initials on a monogrammed gift, it's perfectly acceptable—and easy—to do so. In the case of Ellen White and Andrew Brown, the wife's first and last initials would precede her husband's: EW & AB.

Antiques or Furniture

Consider giving your daughter a family heirloom—whether it's the cedar chest that belonged to your mother or the bracelet that belonged to your wife's grandmother.

No antiques of your own? Buy the couple a refurbished clock dating back 100 years, or an old-fashioned chest of drawers. Something that has already weathered the test of time is always an appropriate and meaningful wedding gift.

But you hate antiques, you say, and so does your daughter. All right. How about a new sofa for the newlyweds, or a kitchen table that will last until they're ready to pass it on to their own kids? Maybe they'd love to have a good desk or a coffee table.

Don't be afraid to consult with them to make sure you pick the *right* piece of furniture—after all, this is something they'll end up living with and looking at day in and day out, hopefully for many years to come. If you want to surprise them, consider surprising them with the *opportunity* to choose an item for their home. If you choose wrong, it will be an expensive mistake.

Get Away!

Of course, you don't have to give the newlyweds something that they can unwrap. If they're putting every penny they have into their wedding, there may be precious little left for their honeymoon. You can step up and save the day—or at least part of it—by contributing to their honeymoon fund.

You can set up an entire honeymoon fund for them through your travel agent. If other family members are at a loss for a gift, they can contribute to the fund and defray the cost. However, if you're the one who has initiated this idea, you'll have to pay the balance. You wouldn't want to stick your daughter with that bill.

Another way to help out in this arena is to call in any favors from friends with great vacation homes. If you can help the happy couple pare down the cost of a getaway, they may suddenly feel as though they *can* afford it.

 FACT

> If you've been sitting on your frequent-flier miles or if you have connections in the travel industry, now's a good time to put them to use. Finagling a deal for cut-rate tickets for the newlyweds alleviates a lot of spending stress for them, which is a great gift in itself.

The Gift of a Friend

Has the bride been a little down in the dumps because her very best friend—the one who grew up next door to your family, the one who still talks to your daughter on the phone all the time, the one you can't imagine *not* being there—can't make it to her wedding? Too expensive, the friend said; she's sorry but she just can't afford the travel expenses.

How about getting in touch with the friend yourself and flying her into town for a few days? Imagine your daughter's elation when she sees her pal, and imagine how grateful she'll be that you thought of helping out in this way. If the friend can pop in a few days before the big event, she can help the bride pull together any last minute details and really feel as though she's part of the wedding, too.

 ESSENTIAL

If you decide to pull off a stunt like this, try to arrange for the friend to arrive early enough so that she and the bride actually have a little time to chat; your daughter will be far too busy on her actual wedding day to have any girl talk.

A Little Pampering

If you've already gone over and above what you wanted to spend on this wedding but you still want to treat the newlyweds with a little something or other, consider a gift that's more of a gesture than a timeless treasure.

When the newly married couple retires to their hotel room (or to their own home) for the evening, surprise them with a basket of goodies. Chocolates and champagne, along with crystal champagne flutes, will be a welcome sight for their tired eyes. If the reception is an afternoon cocktail affair, consider springing for room service so that the newlyweds can indulge in their wedding night dinner with reckless abandon. (In other words, they can order the lobster and *still* go on their honeymoon.)

If they're taking off for their honeymoon from the reception, consider arranging for a wine basket to meet them at their final destination, or arrange for an array of goodies to meet them at their own door when they arrive home. Weary travelers melt at the sight of tasty snacks and good wine.

Big-Ticket Items

All right. So you're willing and able to shell out some serious bucks for the newlyweds. Their needs are obvious to you—they need a house, they need a car, and they need unlimited spending power for the next year or so. How far are you willing to go to nudge them into the realm of Comfortable Living?

Home Sweet Home (You Hope)

Obviously, if you're financially secure enough to be thinking about purchasing a home for your child, you're a pretty savvy guy. If you've bought everything for your kids throughout their entire life, then the purchase of a home for your little girl and her new hubby may seem like an appropriate wedding gift, and one that no bride in her right mind would turn down.

Of course, you'll need to take your daughter's personality into consideration before you sign a contract with a realtor or a builder. Is she very particular—and on issues you can't always predict? You may be dying to surprise her, but a house is one thing many women (and men) just have to choose on their own. The wrong kitchen cabinets can drive a homeowner nuts; the wrong location might mean an extra-long work commute; the wrong layout might mean that the newlyweds will pick up and move within a year.

 ALERT!

> If your daughter has always been easy to please, she may well be thrilled with any home you choose for her, but if there's any doubt in your mind, it's best to touch base with her before you buy. You can't exactly return the property if she isn't happy with it.

Once you decide you're going to buy her the house, any real estate agent or mortgage broker will walk you through the process, but generally speaking, you'll need to enter into a contract to buy the home. You'll transfer the deed to the happy couple, they'll live happily ever after, *and* they'll be the envy of all of their friends.

Helping Them Pay for It

You're not into buying a new home for the newlyweds, but you would like to help ease their financial burden *or* simply make it possible for them to get a mortgage. Coughing up a big lump sum toward their down payment is a grand gesture, and something they won't forget. There are some caveats here, though (as you knew there would be).

For starters, name *your* price first. You want the kids to be looking at homes that are in their actual price range, so do your homework. While the size of the down payment will affect the amount of their mortgage, it is very possible for homebuyers to bite off way more than they can chew—make sure your daughter and her husband know what they're getting into.

You probably have some kind of idea what they're pulling in; if you're lending them money to buy a house, you're entitled to this information. Their monthly payment on a mortgage should ideally be no higher than 25 to 28 percent of their pretax income—feel free to pass this data along to your daughter and her husband.

Their real estate agent or mortgage broker should be their primary source of information, but any honest real estate agent will tell you that it's all too common for buyers to be approved for a much larger mortgage than they really should have, which often results in larger monthly payments than the homeowners can truly afford.

Gift or Loan?

Something else to consider: Is this money an outright gift, or is it a loan? You'll be required to answer this question (in the form of a letter or affidavit) when your daughter and her husband apply for their mortgage. Most mortgage lenders will be much happier to learn that you have given the kids the money, free and clear, and that they haven't taken on *more* liability in order to come up with a down payment.

 ESSENTIAL

> Many buyers are approved for much more than the advisable amount of credit—in some areas, buyers are given the green light to borrow 50 percent of their income. Bad idea. Remind the newlyweds that life is full of other, nonnegotiable expenses (such as food).

While you may not be planning on charging the newlyweds interest if it is a loan, and you may be willing to wait until the end of time for them to repay you, a mortgage lender will be interested in knowing the details about any loans, even this ultra friendly one, including any payment schedule and/or interest charges and whether it's a demand loan (which basically means that you'll be repaid when you demand the money).

If it is a gift, be aware that there is a federal law limiting the amount of any one gift to $10,000 a year—or else it will be taxed. (Also, you should be aware that if you're giving out gifts of this magnitude, you'll suddenly be surrounded by youngsters who are of no relation to you, telling you how you've always been "like a father" to them.)

Chapter 11
The Bachelor Party

One of the most potentially awkward and painful experiences for the father of the bride is the bachelor party—and it's no wonder. Is it really surprising that you wouldn't really care to see your future son-in-law and his friends involved in such a ruckus? Can you avoid the scene without giving off bad vibes? On the other hand . . . is it all right if you really *want* to go and shake things up with the guys?

The Invitation Has Arrived

Oh, geez. You were hoping that you wouldn't be invited to this thing—or maybe it never even crossed your mind, because you assumed you *wouldn't* be invited—and then . . . it happened. Your name appeared on the guest list. The invitation landed on your kitchen table. You got a call from your son, who's really looking forward to partying with you. The best man sought you out in your office last week to fill you in on the particulars. Is it wrong for you to dread this with every ounce of your being?

You're Not a Bachelor!

You like your daughter's fiancé well enough. The two of you get along just swell over Sunday dinner, and he seems to be a real fan of the professional football team you've been worshipping for the last forty-odd years. Still, when you get the invitation to his bachelor party, two words come to mind: *Bad idea.* Or were those two words *No way*? Or *Yeah, right*?

Many fathers feel the same way—that bachelor parties are really for the groom and his friends, and not only do you not want to be there, you can't figure out why they'd want you there. You certainly don't want to watch the groom feeding money to a stripper, and you're fairly certain that he'd have a much better time if you weren't anywhere in the vicinity.

There are a couple of reasons why the father of the bride is routinely invited to larger bachelor parties. For starters, there's good will. If the groom's friends are inviting everyone they can think of (men of all ages, mind you) to attend this raucous event, they'd probably feel bad about not giving you the chance to join the fun if you wanted to.

 ESSENTIAL

> In the same generation, there are some dads who are real partiers and some who have actually moved past that point in life. Most likely the groom's friends have no idea where you stand on this point, so they've chosen to invite rather than exclude you.

For another thing, many bachelor parties are fundraisers for the bride and groom. Every guest is asked to make a donation that will be passed along to the engaged couple. Your donation, it is assumed, will be fairly sizable.

Can You Skip It?

You are absolutely, positively *not* required to attend the bachelor party. Yes, it's a gathering to wish the groom well, and yes, many of the wedding guests will be there. *You* don't have to be. You're not the host; you're an invited guest, and it doesn't matter if you are the father of the bride. You don't have to go if you really think it's a bad idea or if you know you'll be incredibly uncomfortable. If it's a large bachelor party (and many of them are), you probably won't even be missed—especially after the third or fourth round of drinks.

 FACT

> If the invitation requires an RSVP, let the host know that you have other plans that you just can't change. That's about as elaborate as your cover story should get.

If your relationship with your future son-in-law is already strained, realize that turning down an invitation to his bachelor party could make things worse. He might perceive this as a deliberate snub. In this case, make an effort to pop in for fifteen minutes—very early on in the evening, before the trash starts flying. Make your appearance, wish him well, and say goodnight.

All Right, You'll Go

If you *are* planning on attending the bachelor party, you might be looking forward to having some fun with the guys . . . or you might be feeling uneasy about the prospect of attending.

Generally speaking, the larger the party, the better the chance that you'll feel more comfortable. If the guest list reaches far and wide across generations, there will likely be someone your own age in attendance—and probably a few friendly faces in the crowd, to boot.

Bachelor parties in this day and age are often known to rely heavily on booze and semi-naked women for entertainment. If this is right up your alley, you're going to make a lot of new, young friends at this party. If this sounds juvenile to you, there's always a chance that your future son-in-law and his friends are as mature as you are and that you'll come away from the party feeling as though they're really decent guys.

 FACT

If the party is very small, you're probably going to end up hanging around with the groom, his friends, and his dad. If you think his dad's a barrel of laughs, you're all set. If you can't stand the guy, it might be a long night.

Your Daughter's Furious

Of course, for every father of the bride who cringes at the mention of the bachelor party, there's a bride who rages at the thought of the inevitable debauchery. If your daughter is one of these brides, should you really even consider going to this shindig? Wouldn't attending the spectacle only be endorsing and condoning it?

Pick a Side, Any Side

There are arguments to be made on both sides of the issue. If you go, she may actually feel better about the whole thing because she will assume that her fiancé is not stupid enough to do anything really inappropriate in your presence (she may, however, be giving him *way* too much of the benefit of the doubt). On the other hand, if you're looking for the perfect excuse to stay home, you have it: solidarity. It's much more important for you to side with your daughter than to join in the fray.

 ALERT!

> You can probably play this any way you want; however, if the bride-to-be has a definite opinion (for example, she really wants you to go and baby-sit the groom), try to respect her wishes.

Oh, She's Overreacting

You had a stag; it's a time-honored tradition, a rite of passage, and nothing for her to be so upset about. Geez, what's the big deal?

While it's probably fair to say that some brides are paranoid and much too overprotective of their future husbands (the bride who freaks out if her man even looks in the direction of another female is a good example), it's also fair to say that many women feel this way because they know *exactly* what goes on at bachelor parties . . . and they don't like it. Which is a fair enough reaction, and one that many men simply don't want to validate.

If you've been trying to convince your daughter that she's all wrong on this point, ask yourself how you would feel if your *son* were marrying a woman whose friends were planning a party in her honor in a location filled with half-naked men and lots of booze. Doesn't seem so appropriate when the tables are turned, does it?

Even if you support your future son-in-law in this endeavor, try to understand how your daughter is feeling. She'll sense betrayal if you give her a lecture on the finer points of bachelor parties.

 ESSENTIAL

If you can't side with her on this point, don't say a word. Remember, brides are emotional time bombs. One wrong word—heck, one wrong intonation of a *right* word—could set off a series of catastrophic verbal explosions from her sweet little mouth.

Typical Shenanigans

So what's the big deal, anyway? You had a bachelor party. All of the guys got together, played poker, and watched a girl pop out of a cake. Big deal. Sure, there was the requisite drinking, the ball-and-chain jokes, maybe a stripper, perhaps some gambling. Contemporary brides *long* for those good old days.

It was sufficient enough for men to go out and have too much beer at the bachelor parties of yesteryear. Today's men often feel as though they must consume enough alcohol to kill an elephant, just to get the party going. And though you may not want to hear it or acknowledge it as truth, the use of illegal drugs is not unheard of among the younger generation. (To be fair, you shouldn't jump to the conclusion that *every* young man is under the influence of a controlled substance—you should only be aware that drugs are out there and are part of the culture.)

 ALERT!

The modern-day bachelor party is often an exercise in complete overindulgence. Instead of one stripper, there may be an entire bevy of babes—and depending on the location of the stag, these women may be wearing very little by night's end, or nothing at all.

At one time, the groom having physical contact with the entertainers was frowned upon. Unfortunately, with the popularity of lap dances skyrocketing these days, the groom may have his hands full—although theoretically, by law, he can only look and not touch. His friends will stand by, pay for *more* lap dances for their betrothed pal, and hoot and holler.

These are the little things that drive brides crazy—or drive them to indulge in their own over-the-top bachelorette parties.

Appropriate FOB Behavior

You're a good sport, a fun guy, a man's man, a crowd-pleaser. You wouldn't miss a party for the world, and this one sounds like it's going to be a blast. You can drink these young guys under the table, and you absolutely know how to have a good time. Great. You'll be a hit. Just remember, though, that although you're not acting in an *official* capacity as father of the bride, you can't pretend that you're someone else. (Not even if you wear the fake beard and sunglasses.)

Have *Some* Fun

It's a party. You're supposed to have a good time, you're supposed to be sociable, and you're supposed to go with the flow. Guess that means that anything goes, right? Um, no.

Is it all right to get a little loose, to shake your groove thing, to down an entire bottle of vodka? Yes, yes, and no. And that about sums up the line in the sand. Don't cross it. Of course you should make every effort to have fun at the bachelor party. It would be a complete bore for you to show up, sit on a stool, and watch the beer dry on the bar. But trying to show the younger guys that you've got what it takes to party with them isn't the same thing as being a fun partygoer.

If you still like to have a really good time *all* the time, and this works for you in your life, that's your business. This party, though, is a little different and carries special rules and limitations for you. Remember that you are the father of the bride, and as such, you're the family's representative. You're the CEO, the president, the goodwill ambassador bearing your family's flag.

 FACT

No matter how young you feel, the fact is, you're a bit older than these guys. Most men put the brakes on their party train as they get older and life—including the weight of all sorts of responsibilities—broadsides them. This is one of those times to be responsible.

Know Your Limits

Of course, every family is different. If you're the most subdued member of your clan, you've pretty much been given the go-ahead (by your kin) to do whatever you want, because nothing you do could embarrass them. On the other hand, if your wife, your kids, and your parents all wonder aloud time and again when you're going to stop acting so crazy, your future son-in-law's bachelor party is not the time to demonstrate that you can *still* do an upside-down funnel or that you're an exhibitionist at heart.

If you know you love to get nutty at a good party, don't even get started at this one. Think of this as a pre-wedding event—which it is, after all. Many of the same people will be at your daughter's wedding, and she does not want to spend her wedding day hearing about how out of control you were at her husband's stag. You also don't want to show the groom up at his own bachelor party. That's just bad manners.

Wet Blanket Syndrome

So what's a father of the bride to do when he's at his future son-in-law's bachelor party, trying to keep himself under control—and yet, also going with the flow—and the best man offers him narcotics? Or he's pelted with Jell-O shots? Or his eyes are assaulted by the sight of two female "dancers" making out with each other? You know, you're all for fun, but enough is enough, and quite frankly, what you're seeing has exceeded every one of your lowest expectations for this evening.

In the case of fun running amok, is it all right for the father of the bride to step in and call a halt to certain activities? Sorry. No. Not unless you see your daughter's future husband is engaging in certain illegal or immoral activities—he's about to be family, so *he's* fair game. Everyone else is over twenty-one (you hope) and you're not *their* dad. Yes, it's all right to be disgusted with the Sodom and Gomorrah atmosphere—but the churning in your stomach is your cue to get out.

Don't Judge a Groom by His Stag

Say this out loud: *Bachelor parties are often wild parties.* Wild. No matter what goes on at a bachelor party, though, it's important to keep it in perspective. Though the rest of the world doesn't exist in a vacuum, bachelor parties sometimes do. Even the most trustworthy guy in the world can get caught up in the frenzied atmosphere of a stag party—and he can end up doing things he normally wouldn't, and maybe things he would never have dreamed of.

 ESSENTIAL

Regardless of what you think of this tradition, it's his party and he'll get loaded if he wants to. He's presumably an adult, making his own choices, so it would be very wrong for you to make him feel as though he's a child.

Party Pooper!

You're a dad, through and through. You quit all that foolish behavior years ago, or maybe you were never much of a Good Time Charlie to begin with. Somehow, though, you've been talked into going to this bachelor party. You have no intention of engaging in the tomfoolery that typically goes on, and you just know that your future son-in-law won't, either.

Hold on. You can't impose your rules of good

conduct on the entire world. While it's admirable for you to want to hold your daughter's fiancé to a high standard . . . this is his bachelor party.

 FACT

> If there's a time to cut a guy a little slack, it's during his bachelor party. Think about it: Is it really fair to plop this young guy down in a bar, throw free drinks at him, stick a stripper on his lap, and expect him *not* to get pulled into the free-for-all?

If you can't hold your tongue, leave. Or don't go in the first place. And though it's always advisable to give someone the benefit of the doubt and to expect the best of him, this is not the time to hold hard and fast to those beliefs. Expect *less* than the best. At the very least, you won't be disappointed in him, and in the best-case scenario, he may rise above the occasion and emerge a veritable hero (at least in your mind).

Not His Fault

The groom seldom has anything to do with the planning of his own bachelor party, and so the blame and judgment for much of the party rests squarely on his friends' shoulders. Of course, the groom is responsible for his own behavior. It's fair to say that he shouldn't be kissing a strange woman at his bachelor party; it's unfair to say that the strange women shouldn't have been there at all. He didn't invite them, remember.

Other things the groom isn't responsible for:

- The location
- The behavior of other guests
- The cost (donations are sometimes requested)

The father of the bride who really isn't crazy about the son-in-law in the first place needs to be especially careful not to jump to any judgments here. It may be this dad's first instinct to heap the blame for everything about the bachelor party on the groom (because you just *knew* this guy wasn't good enough to marry your little girl). Not fair. The groom has simply been asked to show up, just like you.

 ESSENTIAL

You may be cringing at the thought of stepping into the dive where this party is going to be held—just remember, the groom didn't pick the place. He's the guest of honor, sure, but the key word here is *guest*. He has no more control over the particulars than you do.

Of course, one could argue that the groom's friends are pretty shady characters if they threw together such a distasteful bachelor party. That may be giving them more credit than they deserve. As upright and moral as you are, you could plan the same party just by opening the phone book. They need not have connections in the seedy part of town in order to hire untamed strippers.

Yep, *That's* His Fault

So the groom didn't plan the party. You're willing to concede that point, and to overlook the fact that the bar you're standing in smells as though it doubles as a restroom. You can just throw your shoes in the trash when you get home.

However, you are not willing to let other things slide—such as the fact that your daughter's fiancé disappeared a while back and has just emerged from what appears to be a backroom with another woman. Or perhaps he's more bleary-eyed than he should be after simply ingesting beer, which he claims is the *only* substance coursing through his veins.

While you shouldn't be too quick to judge a groom at his own bachelor party, and while some of this may be situational (i.e., things he never would have done if he were not surrounded by temptation), if you have some very valid concerns, you are absolutely within your boundaries to address them with the man who's about to marry your baby girl.

So how does the confrontation go? That's up to you. In the case of the groom who is dumb enough to be canoodling with another woman while you're in the building, you're right to be furious, and you're absolutely within your rights to call him on his behavior right then and there, as long as he is crossing an obvious line. (Giving him heck for *speaking* to the stripper is going too far.)

 ALERT!

It may be difficult for you to have it out with him, especially if you really like him and he's always seemed like a trustworthy fellow, but this is your duty as the big cheese and chief protector in your family.

If you'd rather wait until he's sober and alone, that's all right, too. You might make more of an impact on him if you approach him one-on-one, instead of trying to speak to him in a room full of revelers.

Should You Spill Your Guts?

Of course, when you arrive home, you'll likely be asked all sorts of questions—by your daughter, if she's there, and surely by your wife. How honest you choose to be is completely up to you, and is probably largely dependent on how upset you are. However . . .

Does your daughter need to know about a groom who has blown his image—at least in your eyes? That's a toughie, and it depends on the infraction. You don't want her getting into a marriage that's going to end horribly due to infidelities or substance abuse; on the other hand, this could really be a case of a groom crossing a line he's never crossed before and would never cross again.

No matter the situation, it couldn't come at a worse time than in the weeks before the wedding. The bride is bordering on an emotional meltdown right now *anyway*, and on a more practical note, everything has already been paid for. Is there enough time to drop this bomb and have the air cleared before the wedding day?

 ALERT!

> In the case of a cheating groom, the money doesn't matter. She should absolutely know. Give the groom a choice: He tells her, or you will. Include a deadline. You can bet that this *will* come out one day, and if she finds out that you knew, it won't be pretty.

If the groom has been opening his mind with some illegal substances, it's almost a sure bet that your daughter already knows this (though she may not admit it to you). If she honestly *doesn't* know it, chances are that the groom really isn't an addict—because she *would* know that. Either way, you're within your Dad Boundaries to let her know. It's her ballgame after that.

Good, Clean Fun

Not all bachelor parties involve nakedness and booze. Your future son-in-law might have incredibly respectable friends and/or relatives who are looking to host a squeaky-clean bachelor party for him. How will these gatherings differ from the traditional stag? For starters, you can breathe a sigh of relief if strippers and belly shots aren't really your thing.

Guess Who's Coming?

The guest list for the kinder, gentler bachelor party may be scaled down somewhat to include only the groom's closest friends and family members. Mere acquaintances, coworkers, and neighbors of the groom will probably be eliminated from the guest list, since this party is really geared toward allowing your future son-in-law to be honored by the people closest to him. The nice thing about this kind of get-together is that it's *planned* to be appropriate for even the most conservative and/or innocent-minded invitees, so if you were worried about how the bride's eighty-year-old grandfather would fare at a traditional stag, you can stop fretting.

In Search of Male Bonding

While you may not approve of young men overindulging in alcohol, you might be amazed at how eliminating excessive booze from the equation makes a party drag, especially when all of the participants don't know each other well. The planners of a low-key bachelor party might decide, then, that dinner in a nice restaurant might be just the thing to keep everyone entertained for a couple of hours while celebrating with the groom-to-be. If the group is really on the small side, the host might shoot for an outing like golf, or an afternoon of deep-sea fishing, or a poker game. A mellow bachelor party needs an activity that allows everyone to talk, but also one that keeps everyone busy so that there aren't a whole lot of awkward silences—*nothing* kills a party faster.

 FACT

> Don't expect a complete moratorium on alcohol. Some guests will expect to imbibe, and it is a party, after all. Having a drink or two can also help guests to feel more comfortable with each other, especially if they've never met before.

Talk the Talk

Limit the amount of your conversation that directly deals with the wedding—unless the groom wants to hit all the high points of the plans. This is supposed to be a night for the guys to talk, and since it's a small group, this is a great time for everyone to really get to know each other. Not only will your family benefit from learning more about the groom, you'll also have the chance to really talk with his family and friends. You'll all be seeing each other at the wedding soon enough—

wouldn't it be more fun to view them as friends during the reception than as strangers?

Talk about work, hobbies, sports, vacations, anything that opens the door to various points of view and further conversation. You want to help keep the conversation rolling, so try to have some topics for discussion at the ready, and try not to sound too rehearsed if you're forced to pull some of them out.

Going Coed?

Oh, no. You weren't even happy when colleges went coed, and you're not about to condone a coed bachelor/ette/family get-together. You're not doing it. You just won't hear of it. It's silly. Girls don't play poker.

Oh, lighten up. If it helps, you can think of this as a delayed engagement party. Going coed takes the strain off of you (if you happen to be a reluctant guest to the bachelor party), anyway. Sure, you'll be expected to partake in some male activities (like the aforementioned card game, or a rollicking discussion of women's driving and/or shopping habits), but the women will probably be planning activities for *everyone*. In addition, with more guests and another gender present, keeping the conversation going will be a breeze. You can also bet that a coed, cofamily bachelor/ette party will not be a wild affair, so if you were concerned about anyone losing their heads, you can rest easy now.

Chapter 12

Wedding Day and Beyond

The day has finally arrived! Are you happy, or are you feeling something that you just can't identify and dealing with it by yelling at anyone who crosses your path? It's completely normal for a dad to feel a little sad on the day he's giving his daughter away . . . but it's also completely normal to be looking forward to a beautiful ceremony and reception. She'll be leaving you now, but if you play your cards right, this may be the beginning of an even better relationship between the two of you.

Wedding Bell Blues

Believe it or not, most dads feel a little sad when they're forced to give their daughters away at the altar—even the dads who never expected to feel the slightest twinge of melancholy. It's really no surprise, though. In addition to literally kissing your daughter goodbye, her marriage signals something bigger, a major passage of time and a new phase in life—hers *and* yours. You're compelled to look reality in the face and realize that you're *not* thirty anymore, and your daughter is no kid.

You're Not Alone

All of this might be enough to make anyone feel a little long in the tooth and sorry for himself, but *you've* never heard anyone—not your friends, not your male relatives, not even any random guy on a talk show—admit to feeling sad over his daughter's marriage.

Well, that's 'cause they're men. And even if some male icon—a football coach or a real man's man action hero, or the President himself—were to present these feelings as valid and logical, many average men would just shrug and say, "Not me. I never felt that way." This is not to say that men are so hardheaded that they won't admit when they're feeling sad about something, such as a child's wedding (though this may also be a valid argument in some cases). Generally speaking, men (even in this day and age) are simply not raised *or* encouraged to express their feelings, even to themselves.

Are you supposed to break down every barrier and express every emotion you're having, the second you're experiencing it? No. That would be swinging way too far to the opposite extreme. You simply need to know that what you're feeling is normal, and that you are not the only father of the bride who has moments when he wishes he could turn back the hands of time.

 FACT

Take time to really sit down and think about how you're feeling. Admit it to yourself, and then you can work through it. Leaving those feelings scattered around the corners of your mind could lead you to feel stressed out without knowing *why*.

Nothing Bothers You

Take stock of yourself. Is your wife always wanting feedback from you, only to hear you say, "Whatever. Anything you want is fine with me"? When you disciplined your young kids, did the expression on your face *ever* change? When something major happens in your life—the loss of a loved one, or a huge promotion at work—do you feel . . . anything? Do you express it?

Some tips for getting a handle on your emotional state:

Acknowledge the hugeness of the day. This is it. Really. No matter how long your daughter's engagement was, no matter how young she seems to you, this is the day she's taking the plunge into marriage. Take some time to let that sink in.

Express yourself. Even if you're not given to showing emotion, don't bottle it up. You might end up seeming cranky or out of sorts, and that's not the image you want to project now.

Pull it together. Once you let those emotions fly, let them land, too. Your daughter is counting on you to be her rock in the weeks, days, and moments before she takes her vows. Get ahold of yourself well before you leave the house for the ceremony.

You want to hit some happy medium between being expressive and being overly emotional, especially on the day of the wedding. No bride wants a zombie dad walking her down the aisle, but on the other hand, no bride wants to be upstaged by a father who's hysterically crying his way to the front of the church.

If an overwhelming sadness hits you all at once on her wedding day, you'll have a fine balancing act to pull off. It's all right to give into that feeling—a little. You *don't* have the go-ahead to mope your way through the reception. If you've ignored those feelings until today, put off *really* expressing them until tomorrow. Your daughter is happy. *Let* her be happy. You can brood all you want when she takes off for her honeymoon. Add this to the long list of things you've suffered through for her.

Get Ready, Man

You're really not sad, you say. You're actually feeling pretty excited about your daughter's wedding day. She's found a great guy, after all, and you're going to reconnect with a lot of friends and relatives you haven't seen in ages. Plus, you look pretty dapper in your tux and you can't wait to boogie the night away. If you've never acted as father of the bride before, you may be surprised to learn that you're going to be a busy little bee on the day of the ceremony—and if you're not careful to slow down and smell the roses, you might wind up feeling as though you missed something. Or everything.

 ESSENTIAL

If it's at all possible, try to sit down and have a cup of coffee together. She may be too nervous to eat, but she'll get your message loud and clear—you know that this is the biggest day of her life (so far, anyway), and you're there for her.

Before the Ceremony

Ah, the hours before the wedding. The day starts out simply enough, but as the time for departure draws near, the atmosphere of your home will become charged with excitement and maybe a little anxiety (or maybe a lot). Before the bridesmaids pull into the driveway, before your daughter gets herself all gussied up, try to make some time to talk with the bride. Ask her if there's anything you can do. Tell her how happy you are for her. Tie up any loose ends now. Once the day gets cooking, her mind will be on other things—like her hair, her nails, her honeymoon.

Invasion of the Maids!

Once the bridesmaids start arriving, you'll likely be pushed aside. It really is their responsibility to help the bride prepare for the ceremony—though sometimes they do nothing more than fight each other for space in front of the mirror; still, traditionally speaking, this is a time when the women are busy preparing themselves for the ceremony, so you can reasonably duck out of sight and get yourself going.

You should have had a haircut at least two weeks prior to the big event, and you should absolutely be clean-shaven (or, in the case of the bearded father, neatly trimmed up for your big scene, gliding down the aisle).

 ALERT!

Neatness counts today. Don't forget to take care of your hands, too. You'll be shaking hands all day long. Make sure your nails are clean, and slap on some moisturizer for good measure.

If you tried on the entire tuxedo ensemble when you picked up your duds, you should be all set. Once you're dressed, have someone else—preferably your wife or a brutally honest daughter—give you the once-over. Is your cummerbund on correctly? Is your tie tied correctly? Any loose threads or hairs on your jacket? Any scuffs on the shoes? There's really not much more to preparing yourself beyond this.

Picture Time

When the photographer arrives, your presence will be requested in several scenes. Then you'll be excused and the bridesmaids, again, will take your place. This is fine and good. Less is always more.

When you're posing for pictures, try to come off looking happy—but *natural*. If you've suffered the agony of appearing rigid or just plain goofy in pictures all of your life, start practicing your smile well in advance of the wedding day. It's bad enough to look weird in the pictures that are upstairs in a shoebox; a bad likeness captured for posterity in a wedding album is something that will follow you forever.

Practicing a smile sounds ridiculous and vain to you? Maybe it is, but if you've *never* taken a good picture, the reason for this could be as simple as your not knowing what you look like when you're showing your pearly whites. Maybe you *shouldn't* show them. Maybe opening your mouth wide enough to show both rows of choppers has the unintended effect of making your eyes look squinty and your cheeks appear rather chipmunk-like.

Tinkering with your smile—in the privacy of your own bathroom—*could* improve your appearance on film. (Will it still seem ridiculous and vain when everyone tells you that you look like a movie star in the wedding pictures?)

 FACT

> Though your own family will probably grow tired of the album in due time, your daughter's friends will see it sitting on a bookshelf and pull it out. No one will comment on your enigmatic expression, but they'll all think, "Huh. I don't remember her father looking so . . . squirrely."

The Longest Ride

If a limo has been heralded to whisk you and your daughter to the church, you're in for a trip like no other—and not only because some strange man is driving. The ride to the church can be nerve-wracking, or it can be fun, or it can be completely silent. You won't know until the wheels are in motion. This is the time to take a look at your daughter and try to determine how she's holding up.

There's no way to even guess how she might feel until the actual day of the wedding—some brides, even those who have been incredibly difficult during the months of planning, acquire an ethereal calm on their wedding days. Other brides, including some who have been easygoing and pleasant in the months leading up to the big day, completely lose their minds when they step into their wedding gowns.

Your job is to respond to her emotional state and to make the best of it. If she's happy, you're all set. If she's nervous or sad or she's on the verge of some sort of breakdown, your task will be a little harder. What's a dad to do in this situation?

- Follow her lead. If she tells you she'd rather not talk, don't force it.
- Calm her. If she's nervous about her appearance or the reception, tell her everything is going to be perfect.
- Don't get mushy. The last thing a faltering bride needs is *encouragement* to cry.
- Crack a joke or two . . . so long as your attempts at humor don't agitate her further.

 ESSENTIAL

Don't lose your temper with her, even if her behavior is bordering on bratty. This creature is not *really* your daughter. She's a bride today, and the differences between the two could fill a book. Be an unconditional rock for her, and know that she will come back down to earth fairly soon.

If all of this fails, hold her hand and sit quietly. Some brides are just frazzled, and there's precious little that will calm their nerves.

The Ceremony

You'll stand with your daughter in the back of the church as the music starts and the bridesmaids process down the aisle. What do you say? You have to say *something*, don't you? This is it, after all. She came in this place as a daughter and she's leaving as a wife, and you have to tell her . . . *what*?

 ALERT!

Don't force yourself to come up with something sentimental and pithy if that's not your style. Letting the moment just be will seem much more natural to both of you.

Keep It Real

You can say whatever you want, including nothing at all. If the feeling strikes you, or if you've been saving a little line for this occasion, lay it on her. Most brides can repeat verbatim what their dads said to them as they waited to walk down the aisle—but the bride with a silent dad will remember that her father held onto her a little tighter than she expected, or that he smiled brilliantly at her before they started their journey.

If you don't normally tell her that you're proud of her, or that you love her, or that you're really happy for her, this is a great time—the perfect time—to express those feelings. If you can say something that will knock her socks off at this moment, she'll add that to her list of Perfect Wedding Day Memories.

The Hand-Off

Once it's your turn to make your way down the aisle, remember the lessons you've learned from the rehearsal and from practicing your smile for the wedding pictures. Don't feel as though you have to keep a stoic face here—smile all you want, nod to so-and-so over there. This scene is as much about you as it is about the bride.

 ESSENTIAL

If you're asked to sit further back than your ex-wife, *don't take offense*. It's standard etiquette practice, designed to keep sparring parents at an arm's length from one other, and also to give the bride some peace of mind.

At the end of the line, of course, a nervous young man will be waiting for you to give him your daughter. Don't rush this. This is not just a symbolic transaction—

you are literally passing your daughter off to another man, who is expected to love and care for her for the rest of their lives, so don't just shove her in his general direction and scamper off to your seat. Shake his hand firmly; give him a word of encouragement; kiss your daughter.

Now you can sit, in the first row of seats if you and her mother are married, in the third row if you're divorced.

Hey! What About Mom?

Funny thing about mothers of the bride. They often spend every bit as much time as the bride does planning the wedding, and then on the day of the event, they're pushed aside by tradition in favor of the bride's dad, who takes center stage along with the bride in church and in the traditional father-daughter dance at the reception. Of course, everyone knows when a particular mother of the bride is the ringleader and grand poobah of the entire day. Still . . . it doesn't seem fair that she isn't a star of the show, like you are. What can you do to make this day special for her?

Talk to Her

She may be every bit as nervous and uptight as the bride is, worrying about whether the caterers will show up on time, how the bridesmaids will act during the reception (no one likes a drunken maid of honor, you know), and how long the priest will ramble on during his homily (the forecast is for high humidity, and the guests will be antsy to get out of church).

Ask how *and if* you can help. Just as your daughter isn't really herself today . . . neither is the mother of the bride. Some moms live by the mantra, "If you want it done right, do it yourself." For example, don't jump in and sign for the flower delivery if you have no idea what it's supposed to include—but *do* offer to help in other areas while your wife takes care of her business. Are there any phone calls that need to be made? Does she need anything from the store? Is one of the bridesmaids stranded on the side of the road, in desperate need of a lift?

 FACT

> These are the things that fathers of the bride are sometimes tasked with on the day of the wedding—housekeeping items. Think of yourself as the Get It Guy. Be accessible to your wife, and to your daughter, too, so that your wife doesn't have to constantly relay the bride's requests to you.

Be Affectionate

In the excitement of the whole day, it's easy for you and your wife to lose sight of the romance that surrounds any wedding. Take the time to dance with her, to tell her how beautiful she looks, to hold her hand while the two of you exit the ceremony site. Go the extra mile and pull out her chair for her at dinner or fetch her a fresh drink from the bar (she's going to need it). Remember, as much work and stress as this wedding has meant for you, it's probably been *more* time-consuming and labor-intensive for her. She has a show to run today, so step in and let her know she's doing a great job and that you'd marry her all over again.

Hello, Madame Ex

If you're divorced from the mother of the bride, your daughter's wedding might just bring out some feelings about your ex that you don't know what to do with—sadness, regret, a lingering contempt for the woman . . .

Whatever the case, your time together produced the lovely young woman in the big white dress, so hold your tongue and do your best to be pleasant. If the divorce was amicable, your experience will probably be fairly typical—you'll say hello, make small talk, share space around the bride. If the separation was about as bad as it possibly could have been, you might feel uncomfortable making pleasant chitchat with your ex.

It's your duty to put your best game face on and be pleasant to everyone—even to your former spouse. Say hello to her, provided you can do so without scowling. Even if you haven't spoken in eons, a simple "hello" is *really* all that's required, especially if the situation is decidedly bitter. You're a mature guy, remember, and the cohost of this event, so pull it together for the sake of the bride.

It's Party Time!

When you arrive at the reception, you'll be expected to take charge and welcome the guests. This is often the most enjoyable part of the entire day—everyone's more relaxed by this point and looking to have some fun—so dive in and get the party going.

 ESSENTIAL

> Thank people for coming, tell them how nice it is to see them, point out the location of the bar and the appetizers. You'll be surprised how easy it is to bounce yourself all over the room once you get started.

Work the Room

While the bride and groom will stand in a receiving line to greet the guests as they arrive, you are not required to join them. In fact, it's preferable if you don't. You can much better serve as host if you're actually *at* the party, which means that the minute you enter the reception hall, you're on. You need to be talking, shaking hands, greeting guests as they walk into the facility. Don't get caught up in an hourlong conversation with your business partner—the one you see every day—until you've had a chance to move about the room and say hello to everyone.

To the Bride and Groom

If you're going to give a toast before dinner, make sure it's appropriate to the occasion. While you want to obviously acknowledge your beautiful daughter, you *have* to say something nice about her husband, too. A nice touch might include a word of thanks to anyone who helped out with the planning, such as the groom's parents; you might also want to acknowledge the merging of the two families.

 ALERT!

> Have some notes at the ready if there's even the slightest chance you might forget part of your speech. Nothing's more troubling than realizing too late that you forgot to acknowledge a major player or two (like the newlyweds).

The best toasts are short, sincere, and not ad-libbed. Know what you want to say, say it in as few words as possible, and make sure it doesn't sound false. (*Don't* tell the groom's dad that you really love and admire him when the two of you haven't had two words to say to each other—ever.)

Good Times

After your toast, after dinner, after the cake has been cut, there's still an entire evening ahead of you. You'll probably have a dance with the bride, and one with your wife, before the throngs of well-wishers hit the dance floor. While the hip-hop playlist may not score any points with you or your two boogie-impaired left feet, the band or DJ will eventually slow things down. Seize the opportunity to dance with your wife, or your mother, or your daughter(s). Invite the groom's mother to trip the light fantastic.

 FACT

> If dancing just isn't your thing, make sure you're socializing with the guests. Now's the time to have a good, long chat with your former neighbor, or to introduce folks to each other.

You want to avoid sneaking out for a long, two-hour smoke or seating yourself in the back of the reception hall where no one will find you. This might be the usual stunt you pull at family gatherings, and it may surprise no one that you're missing in action . . . but this is a special day, and you shouldn't don your Invisible Man mask. Besides, no matter how many years you've spent avoiding the family, it's *still* rude.

Winding the Party Down

Your daughter and her new husband are hitting the road, and they'd rather leave the particulars of closing down the reception machine to someone else—you. While the bills have most likely been settled in the days before the wedding, you may still have some business to attend to.

If something was not to the bride's liking (for example, tables were still being assembled as the guests arrived, or the food was cold), don't be shy about voicing your displeasure to the banquet manager and negotiating a price adjustment, *especially* if the issue at hand is stated in the contract. The head honchos in reputable facilities will usually be *very* apologetic and do their best to make things right (by, say, taking ten dinners off of the bill).

There She Goes . . .

Of course, the inevitable conclusion to a wedding is a daughter leaving her parents' nest. This might be a moot point, at least in the literal sense—your daughter may have been living on her own for years, or even in another city—but still, things change once she says, "I do." Once she takes a husband, her priorities *have* to shift. He has to be Numero Uno, now and always, and you . . . well, you have to wish them well and let them go.

Are They Ready? Are They *Happy?*

Regardless of how prepared they are, once they've taken the plunge, your daughter and her new husband are going to have to be ready for married life. Hopefully, each of them is mature enough to know that *real* life—

after the wedding hoopla—is sometimes pretty dull. They've spent months basking in the glow of other people's good wishes and attending parties in their honor. When all of that comes to a screeching halt, newlyweds sometimes feel panicked, as though they may have been enjoying their engagement far too much to realize what they were *really* doing. Whether these newlyweds are honest with themselves, or each other, or anyone else, about these particular concerns is another matter.

So, if you have a daughter who has recently become a wife and she doesn't seem nearly as happy as you—or she—thought she would be, she may be suffering from Post-Wedding Letdown. Does this mean that she wasn't mature enough to get married? Should you start panicking? Was all of the planning and the expense of the wedding for naught?

Probably not. Most likely it simply means that she's entering a new phase of life. Having experienced change during the course of your own life, you know that big transitions are not easy. Don't pry. Let her hang out at your house if she wants to. Don't encourage her to complain about her husband. This will all pass, and she'll come out on the other side happy as a little lark.

They're *Too* Happy

Often, newlyweds find themselves living a perfect life in a perfect world. As a parent with a few years of experience, you know that real life is far from perfect, and that it's only a matter of time before the walls of their little fairytale kingdom come crashing down all around them—or directly on top of them.

 ESSENTIAL

Once your daughter is married, she may seem like a racecar driver who's out of control, careening down a city street and loving the thrill of it. Or you may fear that she and her husband are the ones standing in the middle of the road, blissfully unaware of what's waiting around the corner.

Let them live in their own atmosphere for now. You're 100 percent correct; life will eventually catch up with them. You don't need to throw your two cents in now, telling them how scared they should be, living paycheck-to-paycheck. They really don't need to hear that the apartment they're renting borders on being uninhabitable. They'll realize these things soon enough, and if their wedded bliss can shield them from some of life's unpleasantries right now . . . well, everyone should be so lucky.

Of course, when those walls do come crashing down, your duty will be to hold your tongue and avoid telling them, "I *would* have told you so, but I was too nice."

Your Hopes for Them

One of the hardest things for parents to accept is that their kids are adults. You may have certain dreams for your daughter, and she may have certain dreams of her own, but it's not uncommon for dreams to be put on hold after marriage. Think back to when you were a young man: Were there goals you wanted to accomplish? Did you meet every one of them, or did some of them fall by the wayside when you realized they didn't jibe with your perfect image of married life?

In the end, you must give your daughter credit for the decisions she makes. If she was planning on going to medical school, but has now taken a job to support her husband as he makes *his* way through graduate school, that's her choice. It's not up to you to tell her she's making a big mistake. You're going to have to trust her best judgment, difficult as it may be. The wisest dads know that if they can't say something nice or supportive . . . they shouldn't say anything at all.

 QUESTION?

Should I offer unsolicited advice?
No. Remember, you're an in-law now, and you don't want to earn an adjective like meddling. Stay out of your daughter's marriage as much as is humanly possible.

A Girl Always Needs Her Dad

Now, let's say you've done all you can to encourage your daughter to get on with her own adult, married life. You've held your tongue on many issues when you could have easily shown the kids the error of their ways (knowing full well that they would disregard anything you said at the time), and you've somehow maintained a supportive, loving relationship with your daughter. You should write your own book! You've done it right.

The payoff of letting go of your little girl is that she *will* come back to you—but when she does, she'll be an intelligent, worldly-wise woman, with the capacity to realize that you really do know a thing or two about the ins and outs of life. By encouraging her independence within her marriage, you're opening up the door to a richer, fuller understanding of one another—and a relationship to match.

Planning Guidelines

This timeline pertains to you and the things you may be paying for or involved in planning. Things that pertain specifically to the bride (such as a visit to the hairdresser six months prior to the wedding to try out her up-do) have been left out. Most brides steep themselves in information about their weddings and know exactly when they should be doing what. You, on the other hand, may need a little help . . .

Planning Guidelines

One year to eighteen months prior to the wedding:

- ❏ Determine the wedding date
- ❏ Decide the size of the wedding (guest list) and the formality of the event
- ❏ Set a budget
- ❏ If the wedding is to be held during peak marriage months (April-October), start looking around for a reception site; a wedding site and an officiant; a photographer and videographer; a florist; musicians; and livery service. Be prepared to sign contracts and fork over deposits after you and your daughter have found the right vendors.

Six months to eight months prior to the wedding:

- ❏ Throw or attend engagement party
- ❏ Get the guest list going
- ❏ Attendants will be chosen (important to you if you have other daughters who will be in the wedding, and you're paying for their dresses)
- ❏ Bride orders her dress
- ❏ Bride and groom fill out their registries
- ❏ Honeymoon preparations begin

Four months to six months prior to the wedding:

- ❏ Find a baker
- ❏ Try on and reserve tux
- ❏ Bride and groom should be looking for a place of their own
- ❏ Your wife will be shopping for her dress

Two to four months prior to the wedding:

❒ Invitations ordered (prepare maps or other inserts)
❒ Book hotel rooms for out-of-town guests
❒ Confirm reservations with vendors (two months prior)

Six weeks prior to the wedding:

❒ Invitations mailed
❒ Bride has portrait done for paper

Four weeks prior to the wedding:

❒ Menu is finalized with reception site or caterer
❒ Reception seating finalized as regrets and accep-
tances pour in from the invited guests
❒ Bachelor party

Two weeks prior to the wedding:

❒ Confirm hotel for out-of-towners

One week prior to the wedding:

❒ Contact guests who haven't RSVP'd
❒ Review final details with vendors
❒ Caterer or reception site needs a final guest count

One day prior:

❒ Attend rehearsal dinner

Contracts and Deposits

If your daughter has chosen a wedding date during the busiest wedding months, you'll have to start looking around at various vendors as soon as she gets the ring on her finger. There is sometimes fierce competition for a certain caterer or band—don't let the competitive atmosphere rush your decision and cloud your judgment.

Only sign a contract after your wants and needs have been spelled out *in writing*. Make sure your decision is final; once you sign the contract, you'll be required to put a deposit down to reserve your daughter's wedding date. Most of these deposits are nonrefundable. Deposit amounts vary from vendor to vendor, but you should never be asked to pay anywhere close to the full amount up front. There's something amiss with a vendor who wants all of your money *right now* (when the wedding's a year off).

Also, try to pay your deposits by using your credit card. You'll have a much better chance of getting your money back (in the case of a vendor skipping town or closing his doors) if you put your credit card company on the case.

For Further Reading

In the mood for a little light reading? Here's a list of books and Web sites that contain lots of information on areas that may be of interest to a savvy father of the bride.

Emily Post's Etiquette by Elizabeth L. Post, Emily Post. Harper Collins, July 1992.

While not all of the information contained in this timeless reference on etiquette is required by the average father of the bride, it contains a few pearls of wisdom for everyone.

The Complete Book of Wedding Toasts by John William McCluskey, Lois E. Frevert (Editor). Arden Book Company, January 2000.

Everyone is covered, from the best man to the father of the bride. Pre-wedding occasions are also included, in case you find yourself standing in front of a room full of strangers offering a toast months before the big day.

The Metrosexual Guide to Style: A Handbook for the Modern Man by Michael Flocker. DeCapo Press, October 2003.

A book for the ultramodern, open-minded dad. You've always wanted to be one of the Beautiful People? Here's a guide for creating a life (the right clothes, the right drinks, the right home accessories) worthy of a magazine layout.

Things a Man Should Know About Style by Scott Omelianuk and Ted Allen. Prion Books, September 2001.

Wondering how lookin' good comes so easy to some men? This book has great advice for the dad who wants to look like he was *born* with style.

✍ *www.barmeister.com*

If you happen to find yourself hosting an at-home rehearsal dinner or engagement party, you'll need some good drink recipes. Look no further than this Web site, which lists hundreds of concoctions for your convenience.

✍ *www.smartmoney.com*

This Web site includes advice for first-time home-buyers, a mortgage calculator, and current mortgage rates (just in case you're being hit up for the money for the newlyweds' down payment).

Conde Nast Traveler, Conde Nast Publications.

Is the bride looking for the perfect location for her destination wedding? Hand her this magazine and start packing.

Index

A

antiques, as gifts, 208
appearance
  grooming, 115, 124–130
  weight, 131–134
  see also attire
artwork, as gift, 202
attire
  for bachelor party, 122
  for casual wedding,
    122–124
  for engagement party, 99,
    119–121
  for formal wedding,
    105–106, 116–119, 241
  for rehearsal dinner,
    121–122

B

bachelor party, 56–57,
  215–234
  appropriate behavior at,
    223–225
  to attend or not, 216–221

attire for, 122
coed, 234
expectations at, 100–101
groom's behavior at,
  226–231
typical behavior at, 219,
  221–223
blessing, giving to daughter's
  fiancé, 24–30
B list guests, 155
bridal gown, 74, 92
bridal shower, 55
bride, 1–22
  after wedding, 253–255
  bachelor party and,
    219–221, 230–231
  children of, 166–167
  cohabitation of, 158–159
  dancing with, 108
  discussing budgeting with,
    83–85, 173–174
  emotions of, 48, 65–70,
    242–244
  estranged, 187–189
  expenses and, 78, 80–81,
    142–144
  maturity of, 1–4, 16–19, 20–21